Pursuing Contentment

How to Find Peace in a Chaotic World

SHANNON TISHER

MEDIA.COM

Published by
Illumify Media Global
www.IllumifyMedia.com
"Let's bring your book to life!"

Library of Congress Control Number: 2022912193

Paperback ISBN: 978-1-955043-72-4

Typeset by Jen Clark
Cover design by Debbie Lewis

Printed in the United States of America

For Erik:
Walking alongside you as your beloved has been a joy and an honor.

Contents

Introduction

THE INVITATION

Dear Reader,

May I be honest with you?

I want to be content. I really, *really* want contentment. I feel a little odd writing that; the juxtaposition of the words *wanting* and *contentment* in black and white on a page looks funny. These words are opposites, aren't they? But I *want* to be content.

Contentment is the inner stillness and peace that comes from trusting God. It is satisfaction. Satisfaction in the Lord. Satisfaction in His presence, His goodness, His gifts. It is that illusive, deep, inner calmness of utter dependence and trust. I *want* to want nothing else because I am satisfied with who I am and what I have in Jesus Christ.

I really want to be content.

Do you feel the same?

Do you long for the inner turmoil to be stilled? Do you want the clamoring need for more, more, MORE to be replaced with quiet assurance? Do you desire to rest with confidence in God's tender care, this trait of maturing faith rooted in wholehearted trust?

Perhaps, like me, you want more than a temporary satisfaction, as after a good meal or when "all is as it should be," a deep, abiding, contentment of the soul, a no-matter-what peace and stillness. I would like to invite you to join me on this journey of pursuing contentment.

Easton's Bible Dictionary says contentment "arises from the inward disposition, and is the offspring of humility, and of an intelligent consideration of the rectitude and benignity of divine providence."[1] Contentment grows from the intellectual recognition of our humble standing in the provision of the holy, almighty God who loves and cares for us. It is turning our hearts and minds to willing trust, confident in His tender mercy.

This definition stood in contrast to the messages of contentment I have seen in our culture. I have read several books and articles on the topic that seemed to define contentment as being happy with what you have. Biblical contentment is a state of mind, inward disposition, and focused hope, rooted in God's character.

Why contentment?

Contentment is a kingdom issue. When the spirits of our souls saved by grace do not bear gracious submission to and pleasure in God's will, we belie the gospel we claim to believe. If we are known for turmoil, despair, selfishness, complaining, divisiveness, worry, greed, despair, and irritability, what do we demonstrate about the God we claim to believe in? We are demonstrating less about ourselves than we are about God. If I am tranquil and unflappable under dire circumstances because I trust fully in the God who saved my soul, I am communicating His worth and ability to the world. When we wholeheartedly (though still imperfectly) pursue contentment, we show the world a different way to live. If I do not act in a way that shows God is trustworthy for my earthly circumstances, how do I ever hope to communicate to a lost world that I trust Him for my eternal destination?

Contentment is a matter of the heart. Contentment is peace with God, peace in God, and peace through God. This peace flows from the fountain of full satisfaction and confidence in God. This kind of peace can only come through the regeneration of the Holy Spirit, in the circumcision of the heart. Contentment, like obedience, must be learned. Neither are natural characteristics. And just as we do not get a pass on disobedience because it comes naturally, we do not get a pass on our natural state of discontent either. Both are sin. Discontentedness is sinful because it springs from a prideful heart, from a place of opposition to God rather than submission.

Discontentment can lead to sin: excessive worry, greed, complaining, fretting, covetousness, pride, and so on. However, contentment leads to a greater harvest of the fruit of righteousness: greater trust, a calm witness, unflappability in the face of turmoil. Paul tells Timothy, "Godliness with contentment is great gain," but reminds him to flee evil desires arising from the love of money, but rather, pursue "righteousness, godliness, faith, love, steadfastness, gentleness" (1 Timothy 6:6–11).

Contentment is not lack of difficulty or ease in life. It is not being unaware of the troubles surrounding you. Contentment is equanimity and composure in difficulties. Contentment is "a constant tenor and temper of the heart," or disposition.[2] Not a one-time flash of pleasant mood, but a deep-seated state of the soul. Contentment is a way of being.

Contentment must come through the willing submission of your heart and life to God's full reign. It must be centered on the truth that God is the rightful ruler of your heart and that in His benefi-cent rule there is nothing better than His love.

Jeremiah Burroughs was a Puritan author and preacher who wrote what many consider to be the pinnacle writing on content-ment, *The Rare Jewel of Christian Contentment*. He defines content-ment as "the inward, quiet, gracious frame of spirit, freely submitting to and taking complacency in God's disposal in every condition."[3] The sense in which the Puritans used the word *compla-cency* is not quite the same as ours today. We see the word as refer-ring to smugness, even self-assurance without full awareness of risk. The archaic usage of *complacency* is closer to the Latin root "to please": being pleased with God and being willing to please God. Burroughs uses it to mean well pleased with God's hand. He defines it as looking above our circumstances to God himself, seeing that in God's care we have everything good and wonderful that we need; therefore, all circumstances can be left at God's disposal. Burroughs further says that to learn contentment is the "duty, glory, and excellency of a Christian."[4]

Thomas Watson writes in *The Art of Divine Contentment*, "The gracious spirit is a contented spirit."[5] The gracious spirit is the soul saved by grace, the beneficiary of God's divine work. He argues, "In contentment, you have the first-fruits of heaven."[6]

Before proceeding, I think it is important to note that seeking contentment is not seeking a special level of favor with God. We already have favor with God since we are in Christ. Seeking contentment is living out the established principles of Scripture. When Paul says, "I have learned the secret of contentment," he is not advocating a secret in the sense that there are mystical levels within Christianity only a few achieve. Paul is speaking of how he personally applied the truth of Christ's indwelling strength to himself to learn to be content. Together, we will journey through Paul's story and writings, concentrating on the book of Philippians to uncover this secret. We will look at how Paul applied these lessons to himself.

Paul was steadfastly confident in God. He was fully satisfied with God and with everything God did in his life. Paul was at peace with God. He was thoroughly God's servant and looked to his Master for everything. Paul learned well the lesson of contentment. As Burroughs explains,

> A gracious heart must needs have satisfaction in this way, because godliness teaches him this, to see that his good is more in God than in himself; the good of my life, and comforts, and my happiness, and my glory and my riches, is more in God than it is in myself. . . . But upon this it is, that a gracious heart has contentment, he melts his will into God's . . . and makes his will over to God.[7]

Friends, let us join our gracious hearts in melting our wills to God's. Let us find all our good in Him as we begin together this journey toward contentment. My prayer for you is to learn to delight in God, being so well pleased with God Himself that you become satisfied with Him and Him alone.

Part One

CONTENTMENT IN A COVETOUS CULTURE

ONE

Covetousness versus Contentment

WE LIVE IN A COVETOUS CULTURE. Advertising in America alone is a multibillion-dollar industry, not to mention the billions of dollars these ad campaigns bring in for the various industries they promote. We are bombarded with ads and marketing campaigns from morning to night. While we get blasted with neon, HD, pop-ups, catchy lyrics, and flashy mottos to fuel our covetousness, it is hardly the source. These expensive ad campaigns are not necessary *for* us to covet; we do that on our own. They are intended to tell us *what* to covet.

You do not have to be from modern Western culture to be plagued with covetousness. Every culture is impacted by coveting because it is an issue of the heart. People in every culture look to the world around them and ask, "What should I have that I do not?" Coveting is an issue as old as time.

The first woman, Eve, was living in unimaginable perfection. God had given her the entirety of the garden. Every fruit was hers to enjoy. Genesis 2:9 tells us that every tree was pleasant to the sight and good for food. She had the blessing of a perfect husband. She had sweet fellowship with God Himself as He walked with them in the cool of the day. God had looked at the entirety of His creation and called it very good (Genesis 1:31).

But there was the one thing God had not given her. It didn't take a flashy ad campaign or neon lights to get her attention—just one slithery voice. In his cunning, crafty way, the serpent twisted God's command to look like God was denying her something good, something important, something divine. *God is keeping knowledge from you. He knows you will be like Him; that's why He has denied you this tree. You should have it. You deserve it.*

Eve looked closer. The tree was good for food, a delight to the eyes, and the tree was desirable for wisdom.

James has this to say about desires: "But each person is tempted when he is lured and enticed by his own desire. Then desire when it has conceived gives birth to sin, and sin when it is fully grown brings forth death" (James 1:14–15).

Eve was tempted when she desired the fruit. She looked closer and saw that it was pleasing. She rationalized eating it because gaining wisdom is desirable.

The next verse in the epistle James wrote says, "Do not be deceived, my beloved brothers. Every good gift and every perfect gift is from above, coming down from the Father of lights, with whom there is no variation or shadow due to change" (James 1:16–17).

"Do not be deceived." When God found Adam and Eve after they ate, she claimed, "The serpent deceived me, and I ate" (Genesis 3:13). She was deceived into thinking what God had provided for her was not enough, that she needed more. She looked at the fruit and saw it was good for food, though it was forbidden by God.

"Do not be deceived." Every good and perfect gift in your life has been given to you by your Father. Your life is filled with blessings.

We, like our first mother, are tempted to look at the things God has withheld and desire them. The covetous heart will doubt God and His provision. It thinks, "If only I had . . ."

At its root, a covetous heart believes that God has withheld a blessing. A covetous heart earnestly yearns but does not possess. Most dangerously, it looks at what *someone else*—one's neighbor—

has and yearns for that with an unloving, envious eye. A covetous heart is willing to transgress to obtain, to take from one's neighbor and make it one's own. In the Ten Commandments, God expressly forbids this: "You shall not covet your neighbor's house; you shall not covet your neighbor's wife, or his male servant, or his female servant, or his ox, or his donkey, or anything else that is your neighbor's" (Exodus 20:17).

Why is it wrong to want what your neighbor has?

Jesus lists coveting as one of the evils that come from within us and defile us (Mark 7:20–23). In Colossians 3:5, Paul lists covetousness as one of the traits of the "earthly" self that we, as new creations in Christ, are to "put to death." He adds an interesting descriptor to covetousness, calling it idolatry. In Ephesians 5:5, he also calls coveting idolatry, adding it should not be named among the sins of the beloved children of God. Wanting, desiring, coveting anything God has not given you is idolatry.

Most of the Old Testament prophets deal with idolatry in some way or another because the Israelites were quite idolatrous. They weren't satisfied with the relationship God had called them into and continually went after anything and everything else. Many of them kept the practices He instituted, but the prophets make it clear they were practicing empty rituals hoping to have the best of both worlds. They expected God to be happy with them and protect them for keeping the rituals. Meanwhile, they participated in idol worship and did not follow the law God had given them. They indulged the flesh. They cheated, swindled, and oppressed as a way of life.

Jeremiah was one of the prophets God sent to call His people back to relationship with Him. Through Jeremiah, God tells this wayward people, "For my people have committed two evils: they have forsaken me, the fountain of living waters, and hewed out cisterns for themselves, broken cisterns that can hold no water" (Jeremiah 2:13).

A cistern is an underground water storage tank. Water from a storage tank is prone to contamination of many type; it is not a desirous way of obtaining water. Note, the people hewed for themselves these cisterns. They were acting apart from God's instructions and intent. Furthermore, they were broken cisterns that could hold no water. It doesn't matter how much water you put in; they will never be filled. Our wants are like cavernous holes we seek to fill. Jeremiah is calling the people's lustful idolatry "broken cisterns."

Yet there is God, the fountain of living waters. Flowing freely. Readily available. Fresh. Nourishing.

God's charge against His people is that they prefer the cistern water over Him. They prefer to work at hewing out for themselves these cisterns and working even harder to fill the broken cisterns.

We do the same thing. We forsake God for the temporary pleasures this world offers. We chase lustfully after the things He has forbidden. We work hard hewing out lives that we think will fulfill us, then work harder to fill them with excitement, happiness, satisfaction, and pleasure. But like water in a broken cistern, it all leaks out as quickly as we put it in. We are idolatrous because we prefer this fruitless cycle to the fresh, living water of God. We prefer seeking the good gifts to the good Giver. We prefer the struggle of obtaining to the obedience of trusting and waiting.

When you earnestly desire something God has not given you, especially if it has been given to someone else, *it* (the thing or person you desire) gets exalted to primary importance in your life. *It* displaces God as King. *It* gets exalted as the goal of your life. *It* becomes what you worship and adore.

When we do not obtain what we desire, most of us will begin to believe the problem is with God, not our wants. Discontent becomes our primary character trait as we focus on the coveted thing we have not obtained.

Contentment seeks to trust wholeheartedly in the provision of the good, gracious Father, keeping congruent the beliefs that He cares for His children and that what we have in our lives is what He deems best.

TWO

Evaluating Our Wants

WANT IS A RIDICULOUS DOUBLE-EDGED SWORD. We are hardwired to want. Want creates drive. We want, so we do. We want a career, so we go to school. We want a family, so we marry and reproduce. We want a home, so we work hard to earn the money to purchase one. We want to retire, so we save and invest. We want to make a difference, so we volunteer.

But want steps outside its bounds. Want quickly slides into coveting. Want easily transfers from a good, God-honoring, God-given desire into a self-seeking, self-satisfying, covetous want. We set our wants as "the thing" to cure our ills, make us happy, satisfy us deeply. Usually, it doesn't. The pleasure we receive from a fulfilled want is short-lived and leaves us searching for the next want.

We are cavernous, yawning pits of want that devour and consume without being filled.

How do we restrain our wants to keep them in check?

We must evaluate our wants

Not just what we want, but why. Is the want that drives you given to you from God? Or self? Or culture?

Think about the reasonable want of career, for example: Do you want a career to pay your bills and contribute to the kingdom? Do you want *that* career because you will look good and impress others? Do you want *that* career because you will be rich? Have you looked at someone in *that* career and thought to yourself, *That is the life I want*? Do you want to advance in your career for reasons of power or prestige?

This is true for big wants and little ones. I often want a coffee drink while I am out running errands. I see my favorite coffee shop or smell coffee when I am in a store and suddenly *want* is awakened. On the grand scale of things, wanting a cup of coffee is minor. But pausing to think about why I want coffee before purchasing a four-dollar cup usually quenches the desire.

There is no want too big or too small that doesn't warrant our evaluation. We should examine ourselves carefully.

As we evaluate our wants, when we find desires expressly forbidden by God or belonging to someone else, we know we are coveting. The only response is immediate repentance.

I am careful with the word *like* when I think of my wants. It brings me awfully close to coveting. Thinking of what others have and dreaming how I could obtain something similar can be a very slippery slope. Maybe I wish my kids were *like* theirs. Or I wish my husband looked *like* him. Or I would love to have a vacation *like* that.

The line between "a thing like that" and "that" disappears once the desire takes root. *Like* is just a mental acrobatic trick to make ourselves think we are not coveting. The line between admiration and envy is wafer thin.

What about everything else in the world? If it doesn't belong to someone else and it is freely available for my purchase and usage, is it okay to want those things? Maybe. Maybe not. This is when it is critical to evaluate the "why" behind the want.

Our wants are the fuel that drive us; they motivate us and direct us, either into the presence of God or into the arms of the world. Either we are pursuing God and the character of Christ, or we are pursuing "the desires of the flesh and the desires of the eyes and pride of life" (1 John 2:16). By evaluating what we want and why we want it, we can more easily sort our wants into those two categories.

I see in myself wants that are good and God-honoring: to study the Bible, to fellowship in a community of believers, to see my children walking with the Lord, to foster a marriage that is healthy and loving, etc. But if I look at my "why" for each want, I must make sure it is congruent. Do I want to study the Bible to be closer to the Lord and more like Jesus? Or do I study the Bible to *look* like I am close to the Lord so others will admire me? Wanting to study the Bible to know God and His ways certainly drives me into His presence. Wanting to study so others would see me in a positive light sounds more like the "pride of life."

I encourage you to write out your wants. Make a list. Take your time and be honest. Think of it as a wish list and bucket list in one.

What relationships do you not have that you want? What do you want from the relationships you do have? What do you want from the people in your life?

What minor, or major, purchases do you want to make?

What do you want to accomplish? What skill do you want to learn? Is there an award or recognition you want?

Where do you want to travel? What do you want to experience?

What do you want for your faith walk? Where do you want to grow? What do you want from your relationship with God? What do you want to do *for* God?

Do you want to lose weight? Get out of debt? Get organized? Run a marathon?

What do you want to feel? Do you want happiness, joy, excitement, fulfillment? What do you want others to feel about you? Do you want admiration, respect, honor? Praise, affirmation, recognition? Do you want healing or deliverance? Restoration? Justice? To know that you are loved? Wellness? Wholeness? Comfort? Safety?

Once your list is made (be thorough, but don't expect it ever to be complete), spend some time with the Lord asking why you want what you want. Look deep inside yourself for the motivation. Even with the seemingly God-honoring things, search for the why.

As you pray through your whys, also look for any wants that are contrary to Scripture. Cross out any that are blatant sin. Cross out any that are covetous. If you want anything that belongs to someone else, or the precarious "like someone else's," repent of these desires. Ask God to forgive you for wanting what He has not given you.

Evaluate the emotions attached to your wants as well. Unmet wants that illicit a response of anger, resentment, or doubts of God's goodness are most likely idols you are clinging to.

Also, pay attention to any temptation to obtain a want through less than honorable means. Any temptation to lie, steal, cheat, or sneak your way into a good thing automatically makes it a bad thing. These wants should be crossed off the list as well since the temptation to pursue them is going to lead you into sin.

Ask God to shape your wants to honor Him. Ask Him to remove the desires that aren't His desires for you. Ask Him for patience as you wait for His timing on the wants. He will fulfill in His time.

This isn't a "one and done" exercise. This is a constant, ongoing, lifelong process.

We must intentionally shift our wants

When we start to take charge of our wants, it begins to be plain we want too much and many are the wrong things.

Our covetous culture constantly tries to convince us we need more, bigger, better, newer, shinier, flashier, more advanced, or more luxurious. Whatever the culture is selling right now is the best. Until the next thing comes along. And it will always come along. These hungry wants will gnaw away at our contentment if we let them.

Our culture tells us to dream big, set goals, work harder, take out loans—whatever it takes to fulfill those desires. The culture tells us we can only be happy when we get what we want.

However, we cannot seek to fill the cavernous hole of want and pursue contentment at the same time. They are completely incompatible. We should intentionally seek to want less than our hearts are naturally inclined to pursue, to ignore the messages from our culture that drive the lust for more.

Philippians 4:10–18 provides a glimpse into the wantless-ness of Paul. Having received a gift from the Philippians, he is thanking them for their generosity. He is careful to offer this thanksgiving without looking for another gift. He says he wasn't "speaking of being in need" and thanks them for "sharing in [his] trouble" but assures them he wasn't seeking "the gift." Paul saw that their gift was evidence of God working in them, producing generosity.

Paul was thankful for their generosity because of what it represented *in them*. The gift is "a fragrant offering, a sacrifice acceptable and pleasing to God" (Philippians 4:18). He acknowledges their concern for him, demonstrated in their act of giving.

He was thankful for the concern they expressed through giving. He was thankful for the support they had shown his ministry in the past. After Paul left Philippi, a city in Macedonia, they had given to him multiple times as he went on his missionary journey through Thessalonica. Paul spoke of these brothers to the Corinthians when he was encouraging generosity. He said the Macedonians had given beyond their means, "for in a severe test of affliction, their abundance of joy and their extreme poverty have overflowed in a wealth of generosity on their part" (2 Corinthians 8:1–5).

The Philippian church was not a rich church. Yet their generosity was astounding. Paul's gratitude was because their commitment to the Lord was represented in their commitment to giving. Paul saw their gift as fruit of their faith. *This* was what Paul wanted.

When we survey the "wants" Paul lists in his writings, we see other desires. He wanted the churches he started to be vibrant, growing ministries full of people walking in a manner worthy of the Lord Jesus Christ. He wanted to visit his friends to see their faith in action, to travel to Rome so they could mutually encourage each other; he wanted his friends and the disciples he had made to stand firm in their faith, to have pure doctrine, and to fulfill the law of love. He wanted them to pray for him to have opportunities to speak and more boldness when he had opportunities! The only physical request Paul makes of his friends is for Timothy to bring his cloak, books, and parchments.

Paul's passion for the things of God drowned out the clamoring cry of the world. Paul was so satisfied in Christ that the world's offerings were mere blips on his radar.

First-century Roman culture was not as different from modern America as we might suppose. The list of wants on any average Roman citizen's list would be comparable to any list we might make. Status, affluence, influence, possessions, and luxury were as desirable then as they are today. But not for Paul. His wants were for the Lord and His glory.

We should seek to increase our want for the Lord and the things of His kingdom while we decrease our wants for what the world offers. Our list of wants should be growing to look more like Paul's, less like a department store inventory.

There is a temptation to swing the pendulum the other direction toward asceticism. Asceticism promotes gaining favor with God by strict avoidance of indulgences of any kind. It is a rejection of pleasures. The premise is that by denying yourself *any* indulgence, you can attain a greater spiritual gain. Asceticism puts forth a list of acceptable things to have, do, or eat.

Paul addresses this in Colossians 2: "See to it that no one takes you captive by philosophy and empty deceit, according to human tradition, according to the elemental spirits of the world, not according to Christ" (v. 8). He urges them not to be disqualified by "insisting on asceticism" (vv. 18–19). He reminds them that they have died to the things of the world; therefore, the rules the world lives by do not apply. These rules, he says, "have indeed an appearance of wisdom in promoting self-made religion and asceticism and severity to the body," but they do nothing to stop "the indulgence of the flesh" (vv. 20–23).

The church in Colossae was fighting similar battles as the church in America. The church was beleaguered by religious practices contrary to the gospel. The church has always been prone to syncretism, that is, mixing and matching parts of different religions. This creates an unstable mixture. One of these religious practices infiltrating the church at Colossae was asceticism.

This Greek philosophy—and practice—was common in Paul's time. These man-made ideologies promise reward in the future for self-denial now. You may hear it in our culture put this way: "Nothing tastes as good as skinny feels," or "If you live like no one else now, you can live like no one else later."

It isn't so much the denial of self that is the issue; after all, Jesus tells us to deny ourselves. It is the strict adherence to a list of rules without a change of heart that Paul takes issue with. It has the *appearance* of wisdom and godliness. You can give up everything and live in a tiny cell in a monastery and be far from God. You can still have a lustful, prideful, covetous heart, wanting all the world has to offer. You can still be dissatisfied with God. You can still be discontent.

I will not tell you how much you should have. That is completely between you and the Lord. Telling you to want less is in no way telling you to become ascetic. I am telling you to participate in a lifelong conversation with God about your heart condition; to stop the culture-driven cycle of increasing want; to engage in the process of your spiritual growth and development. As you increase your want of holiness and righteousness, as you learn to be satisfied in God and with God, you will have to intentionally want less of the world. If the cavernous hole of want in your life is filled with the goodness of God, there cannot be room for the things of this world.

The danger of asceticism is rejecting what God has given us to enjoy. The danger of our covetous culture is forgetting that it is God who gives. Paul tells Timothy in his first letter, "As for the rich in this present age, charge them not to be haughty, nor to set their hopes on the uncertainty of riches, but on God, who richly provides us with everything to enjoy" (1 Timothy 6:17). We are to hold firmly to God, while enjoying what He gives.

Then, Paul instructs, "They are to do good, to be rich in good works, to be generous and ready to share" (1 Timothy 6:18). We are to live with open hands. Open to receive the blessings God gives us to enjoy, while remaining open to let the blessing flow freely out to others. Not with grasping, clawing hands seeking to grab whatever they can lay hold of. Not with snatching hands, taking what does not belong to them. Not with closed-fisted refusal to enjoy the bountiful gifts of the Lord. Not hoarding what crosses our palms. Not wanting more than is placed there.

Contentment is wanting God more than anything. It is delighting in God. It is enjoying God. It is seeking Him first, most, and wholeheartedly. By living this way, Paul says, we will "take hold of that which is truly life" (1 Timothy 6:19).

By intentionally and systematically reducing our wants in this world, with the intention of wanting God more, we turn from our idols and broken cisterns. We look less and less to the world to meet our wants. We find in God the true source of joy, peace, happiness, and contentment.

THREE

Reducing Our Wants

DAY IN AND DAY OUT, our wants direct our choices. Our covetous culture tells us to make our plans and set goals based on our wants. Culture tells us we will only be happy and fulfilled if we get what we want.

But our wants are fickle tyrants. Reexamine your own list of wants. How many contrary wants are there? One may want to get out of debt but also want a bigger house, a new car, a boat, and the ability to send their kids to the best private schools. One may want to lose weight but also want a double cheeseburger with fries and a milkshake. One may want to run a marathon but also want to spend their free time watching TV. Which want does one focus on first? Usually, the one that sounds the most appealing in the moment.

Often, it is the little wants that drive us. We see something we want, then forget that we were going to place another's needs above our own, or pray about how we spend our money, or give to the poor. These little choices to indulge or deny our wants begin to define us as Christ followers. We are shaped by the little choices we make. As we think about these little wants, individually they seem inconsequential, but the daily tally shows their impact keeps us from becoming the full-grown, mature disciples we could be.

The solution is to submit every want—even the tiniest of wants—to the Lord. We ask Him to form and fashion everything we desire after His will and His will alone. Again, not following someone else's list or plan. We are not seeking to follow an external checklist but to have our hearts shaped by the Holy Spirit. One way we can learn to submit our wants to the Lord is by denying ourselves.

Paul teaches that, although some may say, "'All things are lawful,' . . . not all things are helpful" and "not all things build up" (1 Corinthians 10:23). So much of what we desire, while lawful, may not be beneficial for our pursuit of contentment. Many of these wants can be considered indulgences or luxuries. We can allow the Lord to shape our wants by prayerfully and intentionally abstaining for a time. This is an especially effective practice if we are replacing the time or money we would spend fulfilling our desires with a thing of God: a spiritual discipline or act of generosity.

As we deny ourselves, we break the power the little tyrannical wants have over us. We can become free to enjoy the good gifts in our lives without being enslaved to them or mastered by them.

After you have denied yourself the good pleasures of this life for a period, there is a time to enjoy them with thankfulness if and when the Lord allows.

I want to issue you a two-part challenge, though.

First, savor the pleasure. Take your time to enjoy the goodness of the gifts of God. Spend time thanking Him for the gift. Whatever you have denied yourself, when you feel God giving you the green light to enjoy it again, enjoy it with gusto. Overflow with thankfulness. See how many individual things about the indulgence you can find to be thankful for. Remember, we are trying to focus our hearts on wanting God more than we want anything of the world. When we profusely thank the Lord for the good gifts He gives, we firmly cement Him in our hearts as the Giver; we turn our attention *from* the good thing we are enjoying *to* the faithful God who gives us all things for our enjoyment. We keep the gifts from becoming wants that rule our hearts. When we look for things to be thankful for as a habitual practice, our eyes are transformed to see the goodness around us as a witness to the goodness of God, as things to be enjoyed rather than possessed.

The second part of the challenge is to bring someone along. Invite someone to participate with you as you enjoy the gifts of God. When we bring others into our joy, when we share our blessings, we are opening our hands to the gifts God gives.

One final thought as I conclude this section on want: most likely, we can look back over the wants we had as children or adolescents and see them as the unrealistic, frivolous dreams they were. One of my most unrealistic desires was getting the lead singer of my favorite band to see me at their concert and fall hopelessly in love with me. It was all I could think of for months leading up to the concert. Eventually, I realized what a bad idea that was (on so many levels!), and now I can laugh at myself.

I think we would laugh at ourselves with the same understanding spirit if we could see our wants from God's perspective. Even big things, good things, things that we think could bring Him glory, might seem foolish to us if we had the benefit of an eternal perspective. We do not have the benefit of knowing the whole story from beginning to end, let alone our own story. We do not know how obtaining the thing we want could cost us, damage us, or endanger us.

Consider Israel. They wanted a king like all the surrounding countries. Samuel told the Israelites what it would cost them. Their sons would be conscripted and become soldiers, and their daughters would be taken to be servants in the palace. The king would take land and tax them heavily. They all agreed the cost was worth it (1 Samuel 8:1–22). But the kings cost the Israelites their unity as a nation, their holiness, then eventually their country itself. King after king led the people into further sin and idol worship, which ended with exile and the destruction of Jerusalem and the Temple.

We do not know what our wants will cost us. We would do well to accept the benevolence of our God who does not always give us what we want. We should accept the mercies of unfulfilled desires because we know God is working for our benefit. I do not know why God has said no to many of my wants; maybe He will reveal the reason someday. I am learning, as I grow in contentment, to want only that which He has given me. I am learning to accept that what He provides is far better—and possibly less costly—than anything the world offers.

FOUR

Paul's Encouragement

BEFORE PAUL CONCLUDES his letter to the Philippians, he gives them one last encouragement: "And my God will supply every need of yours according to his riches in glory in Christ Jesus" (Philippians 4:19).

Paul speaks from a place of great confidence in God's provision. This confidence comes from experience. Paul knew God, knew God's provision, and therefore had unfailing trust in God's ability to meet needs. This verse comes at the tail end of the "thank you" portion of his letter. Remember, the Philippians had sent a financial gift to Paul. He carefully thanked them, not because of the need he had, but because of the fruit their generosity would bear.

Paul claims God's riches. Seems fitting in talking about money to bring up riches, right? In our modern churches, we talk of riches in the "God owns the cattle on a thousand hills" perspective. We reason that if God is rich enough to own all those cattle, He must be rich enough to pay my bills or drop a check in the mail when I need it.

Paul is saying something else, though. He started out talking about money but has shifted to their sacrifice, the spiritual act of their giving. He ties their spiritual act of giving to God's riches. This verse in Philippians is one of thirteen passages Paul writes about

God's riches. He ties these riches to mercy, grace, love, wisdom, forgiveness, and redemption. These are better than mountains of cattle!

Paul asserts the riches of God are of an eternal nature, rather than temporal: the salvation of our souls, the eternal inheritance awaiting us, the glorification of God through Christ Jesus.

Here is the good news: if you are in Christ, you are heir to immeasurable riches. Immeasurable!

You are sealed with the Holy Spirit as a guarantee and a down payment on the inheritance (2 Corinthians 1:22; Ephesians 1:13–14). If you have been walking with the Spirit and have experienced the sweetness of this blessed fellowship, it is beyond imagination to think of what the full inheritance will be like. When we are free from our body of death, when we are no longer tempted to sin, when we see as face-to-face rather than dimly as in a mirror, that will be the most joyous experience beyond our wildest imaginations (1 Corinthians 13:12)!

Paul is telling the Philippians that God will supply their every need. But it is according to the riches of eternal life. Here's the "bad" news: God defines your needs. God decides how your needs will be met. God determines the method for meeting your needs (I put "bad" in quotation marks because it is not actually "bad"; however, this might feel "bad").

God's primary concern for your life is your Christlikeness. Therefore, He will supply all your needs according to *His* riches in glory in Christ Jesus. He wants to refine you. He wants to purify you, to remove sin from your life. He wants to conform you to the image of Jesus Christ.

God is creating for Himself a people worthy of the inheritance they are going to receive.

Maslow versus God

Since Abraham Maslow presented his theory of human needs in 1943, the hierarchy has become common vernacular for any discussion of needs in our society. He theorized we all have the following five needs:

1. Physiological needs: food, water, warmth, rest
2. Safety needs: security, safety; psychological needs
3. Belongingness and Love needs: intimate relationships, friends
4. Esteem needs: prestige, feeling of accomplishment; and self-fulfillment needs
5. Self-actualization needs: achieving one's full potential, including creative activities

Each lower need must be met for an individual to move to the next higher level.[1]

While there is moderate value in using this explanation as a diagnostic where there is dysfunction—an undernourished child may not thrive in education, for example—we have errantly taken this hierarchy as gospel truth.

Paul repeatedly had most of his basic needs unmet. Food? Went hungry. Water? Was thirsty. Warmth? Was cold and exposed. Rest? Toil, hardship, many sleepless nights. Security and safety? He faced danger constantly. Belongingness and love? Paul was rejected by many, abandoned and alone while in prison and on trial. Esteem? Paul was mistrusted, falsely accused, reviled, hated, run out of almost every town; he was criticized, questioned, and insulted by his followers (2 Corinthians 6:3–10; 11:23–28).

Paul said in Philippians 4:12–13, "I know how to be brought low, and I know how to abound. In any and every circumstance, I have learned the secret of facing plenty and hunger, abundance and need. I can do all things through him who strengthens me." Paul knew how to face these different circumstances because he had experienced them.

And yet, he asserts, "My God will supply every need of yours according to his riches in glory in Christ Jesus" (Philippians 4:19). Paul was not saying, "Every need of yours will be met, while I, Paul, am left hungry, thirsty, cold, beaten, and shipwrecked."

Paul is confident that every need of his readers *has been* met in Christ. If you have Christ, you have everything. In giving you salvation, God gave you everything you *need*. Everything else He gives you serves the purpose of making you more like Christ, according to His riches in glory.

Maybe you need hunger. Or thirst. Or friendlessness. Or want. Or persecution. Perhaps having one of Maslow's needs unmet is precisely the tool God will use to meet your greater need to be like Christ. God will use whatever tools He deems necessary to accomplish that end.

Interestingly, when you look at how the Word reveals God, you can see how *in Him* our needs are defined. Jesus is the Bread of Life and Water of Life. God is the Fountain of Living Water. Jesus is Emmanuel, God with us. The Lord is our fortress, our stronghold, and our shield (Psalm 18:2). He is "our refuge and strength, a very present help in trouble" (Psalm 46:1). In Him every need is met.

Sometimes God does not meet what we perceive to be a need to show us what true need is. When Maslow said we need food, water, warmth, and rest, our sinful, selfish hearts interpret that as three full, multicourse meals a day, plus desserts and snacks; water in the form of specialty coffee drinks, sweet tea, soda/pop, etc.; a three-thousand-plus-square-foot house with a fireplace and central heat set to a perfect temperature; and multiple days off a week to "rest" through leisure activities plus eight solid hours of sleep in a comfortable California-king-sized bed. We easily twist "need" into far beyond even Maslow's intentions.

The truth is, even if we were going to have our needs met according to Maslow's hierarchy, we need far less than we think we need. In every category. When Paul said, "But if we have food and clothing, with these we will be content," he was talking of having *just enough* food and clothing, not overabundance (1 Timothy 6:8).

We can rest in His provision, knowing everything we have is from God and for our good and His glory. We have everything we need in Christ, and we can trust our God is a good, gracious, loving Father who will supply our needs.

Trusting God with Our Needs

We looked at denying our wants in the last chapter. Now we are going to look at denying our needs through the practice of fasting.

Fasting is denying yourself a basic need such as food for a length of time for the purpose of seeking God. By giving up food for a time to seek the Bread of Life, we are filled. By giving up water for a time to seek the Fountain of Living Water, our thirst is quenched. It is connecting our hearts back to the truth that our needs are fully met in the sacrifice of Jesus and we have "all things that pertain to life and godliness" (2 Peter 1:3). In Him we also "live and move and have our being" (Acts 17:28). Fasting says, "God, I trust You more than I trust the things I think I need."

Jesus expected we would fast, giving instructions that begin, "when you fast" (Matthew 6:16, 17); I am convinced this is enough of a reason to practice it. Nobody wants to start fasting. In the Old Testament, the Lord gave instructions to fast—the *English Standard Version* (ESV) says to "afflict yourselves"—in relation to several of the holy days. God calls it "afflicting yourselves" for a reason. This is the same root word He used when He said, "I have seen the affliction of my people who are in Egypt . . ." (Exodus 3:7). The affliction of slavery. The affliction of being under harsh task masters. Yet "afflict yourselves"?

Fasting is meant to be difficult. It is meant to be hard. It is meant to be an affliction. It is meant to expose your slavery to your passions and desires. It is meant to reorient you to the righteousness to which you are enslaved (Romans 6:16–19). This is not denial for the sake of denial. This is denial for the sake of seeking the Lord. We replace our meals with prayer and Bible reading. We humble ourselves before the Lord, filling up spiritually in His presence while feeling the effects of physical need in our bodies.

We must practice denial of self before we can journey toward contentment. We will not master our passions in this life, but we can make strides toward that goal. We may wrestle with these desires for the rest of our lives, but thanks be to God through Jesus Christ our

Lord—we will be delivered from this body of death! (Romans 7:24–25).

In my journey toward contentment, addressing my wants and needs opened my eyes to how little I have trusted the Lord. I confess I had let the lie "If God loves me, then He will [fill in the blank]" permeate and poison my heart.

There is no "if" God loves me. If you are in Christ, then you are the recipient of God's love. Period. And *since* God loves you, then you are receiving what He wants you to receive. He is providing for you. Period.

To be content, we must understand God's love more fully. We must set our hearts to searching the Scriptures for evidence of God's love. We must instruct our hearts that God loves us and will always be faithful to us. In the Old Testament, God's character is often described with the phrase "steadfast love and faithfulness." When Moses asked God to show Himself to Moses, so that Moses could know Him and walk in His ways, God did just that (Exodus 33:12–23). The Lord passed by where He had hidden Moses in the rock, and said, "The LORD, the LORD, [is] a God merciful and gracious, slow to anger, and abounding in steadfast love and faithfulness, keeping steadfast love for thousands, forgiving iniquity and transgression and sin . . ." (Exodus 34:6–9).

Abounding in steadfast love and faithfulness. This is much, great, abundant steadfast love and faithfulness.

We have a clearer picture of God's love than Moses because we have the full gospel. We know that "God shows his love for us in that while we were still sinners, Christ died for us" (Romans 5:8), and "God, being rich in mercy, because of the great love with which he loved us, even when we were dead in our trespasses, made us alive together with Christ" (Ephesians 2:4–5). "See what kind of love the Father has given to us, that we should be called children of God; and so we are" (1 John 3:1).

Who, then, am I to question His love as I see it demonstrated in my wants and needs being met in this earthly life? His love was demonstrated in the horrible, costly death of His beloved Son. His love was demonstrated in my own adoption as His child, confirmed by the indwelling of the Holy Spirit.

If we are discontent when we have this gracious, steadfast, faithful love poured out on us, we do not understand this love. When we are discontent because we do not get the things of this world, we do not understand the ways of heaven.

We may know God is the Lord of heaven and Earth, but we need to remind our hearts repeatedly. We may know He loves us, but we need to tell our hearts again. We may know we need to trust God to provide what we need, but we need to remind our hearts again that He will. Again and again. As soon as we start to think, "I know God loves me, but . . . ," we need to return to our knowledge of God's love and reinstruct our hearts to believe it with no "but."

Jesus revealed God as the loving Father. He taught His followers to pray, "Our Father in heaven . . . . Give us this day our daily bread . . ." (Matthew 6:9–13). Jesus also asked, "Or which one of you, if his son asks him for bread, will give him a stone? Or if he asks for a fish, will give him a serpent? If you then, who are evil, know how to give good gifts to your children, how much more will your Father who is in heaven give good things to those who ask him!" (Matthew 7:9–11). Jesus was so convinced of God the Father's loving provision for Him that when Satan tempted Him with stones He could turn to bread, He left the stones as stones. He knew His Father could make bread rain from heaven. Jesus knew that God could supply bountifully anything and everything He asked. Certainly, after fasting for forty days, He wanted to eat; otherwise, it would not have been a temptation. But He trusted the Father's love.

There will be no contentment until we are utterly, assuredly, and completely convinced of God's abounding, lavish love for us. As long as we hold even a miniscule particle of doubt about His steadfast love and faithfulness, we will doubt His provision of our needs and fixate on our unmet wants as a measure of His love. There will always be the temptation to look to the unsatisfying things of the world and value them above God. But in seeking contentment, we must leave the stones as stones and trust our Father's love.

Part Two

CONTENTMENT IN CIRCUMSTANCES

FIVE

In Every Circumstance

INTELLECTUALLY, we know that life is hard. We know bad things happen to good people. We know that sin has permeated every corner of our existence and sometimes we will have our lives tainted by its stain. We know that accidents happen. We know, as the saying goes, that "the only two guarantees in life are death and taxes." We know that Jesus said, "In this world you will have tribulation" (John 16:33). We know these things.

And yet . . .

We experience our share of rough terrain and suddenly we ask, "Why me?" "Why this?" or "Why now?"

But worst of all, we ask, "Why, God?!" When the enemy fires the flaming dart of tempting us to question God, our difficult circumstances cause us to drop the shield of faith and catch the firebrand. We hold it close and nurture the flame. We doubt God's goodness, mercy, love, fairness, justice, and power. In the whispered places of our hearts, we ask, "Where are You? Why didn't You stop this? If You really loved me . . ." We build a case against God. We question His concern for us.

Why do we do this? Here are two possible reasons:

First, as humans, we make decisions. Every day, we each make big and small decisions. From what to eat to what career to pursue, and from what to wear to what house to purchase, our days are filled with decision making. While our decisions can be good, bad, or neutral, making decisions gives us the feeling or sense of being the one in control of our lives. We chart our own course and believe ourselves to be the "master of our own destiny."

So, what happens when things don't go according to plan? What happens when our decisions don't pan out the way we decided they should?

We are left to reckon with our failure. Since we know the logic and reason behind our own decision making, we cannot be the problem. We trust our own gut more than the God of the universe. We set our course and expect God to be on board with our plan. We somehow equate being in control of our decision-making process with being in control of our lives.

Second, there is an undercurrent in modern Western/American churches that insinuates, "I have done something remarkable in accepting Jesus as my Savior; therefore, I deserve to be rewarded." Oh, people may not actually say that, but if you listen carefully, they say it. "He's such a good, godly man. I can't believe something like this would happen to him!" or "She does so much for the church; I don't know why she is going through that!" Or even "What's the use of serving God if this is what I get for it!"

We equate obedience with blessing. Blessing on our terms. Blessing as we see fit. We believe that our personal obedience is remarkable and, therefore, worth great rewards.

This—in and of itself—is enough to breed discontentment. When we think we are entitled to blessing (reward, prosperity, health, wealth, happiness, etc.), we set the standard of what God's blessings look like. However, what God chooses to bless us with is (usually) very different from our imagined reward. This leads us to question God: either He isn't good because He isn't blessing us like He should, or He is incapable of keeping His end of the bargain. We thank God for the things *we* categorize as blessings, yet how easily our thoughts turn to anger when we get circumstances that aren't "blessed." I admit that for years my first thought when I faced difficult circumstances was, *It's not fair! I have done . . .* , and completed the thought with a long list of reasons I should not be experiencing any type of struggle.

The problem with these ways of thinking should be clear. We are not the ones who set the course for our lives, nor the ones who determine what should or should not come into our lives. We cannot learn contentment if we are trying to control our own lives. We cannot grow into content, mature believers without difficulties. We cannot be at peace with God if we constantly expect Him to hold up the end of a bargain He never made. God did not save us to make all our hopes and dreams come true.

The gospel Paul believed and preached was far different from this lie that has permeated our churches. Paul's faith looks more like this: *God* has done something remarkable in loving us, the wretched sinners we are, in not giving us what we deserve; He has given us new life in Christ, and everything He blesses us with is for our good and His glory. Our true blessings include adoption, an eternal inheritance, a new nature, a new heart, forgiveness of sins, redemption, justification, glorification, eternal life, and the Holy Spirit, just to name a few.

Some circumstances feel unbearable. Some feel as if they will crush us. Some circumstances seem more than we can bear. We struggle, walking this earth with burdens. We face trials. We have the consequences of sin to deal with—ours and others'—in small and large ways. We face illness and death. We watch loved ones suffer. We suffer.

In attempting to face our circumstances in the pursuit of contentment, we are not denying their difficulty or using Scripture as a trite way to brush them under the carpet. No. They are real, and they hurt. They are hard.

Paul could relate. This man knew difficulty. He faced circumstances we cannot imagine. He would be very sympathetic to many of the challenging times each of us faces.

And yet, Paul was content.

In Philippians 4:13, Paul gives us a wonderful verse to pull out of context and misquote: "I can do all things through him who strengthens me." This is a favorite verse of marathon runners and Christian T-shirt designers. Yes, it is a great truth with immense power! We must keep it in context, however. Paul is talking about contentment. "Not that I am speaking of being in need, for I have learned in whatever situation I am to be content. I know how to be brought low, and I know how to abound. In any and every circumstance, I have learned the secret of facing plenty and hunger, abundance and need. *I can do all things through him who strengthens me* (Philippians 4:11–13, emphasis added).

You, too, can learn to be content. And you, too, will have to go through difficulties to learn it.

Contentment is deep, spiritual satisfaction in God through the power of Jesus Christ. You must go through circumstances where you must rely on Christ to *learn* to rely on Him. You will never learn what things you can do through Him who strengthens you if you never have circumstances that require His strength.

But, oh what grace and mercy there is in this! It transforms the realities of living in a dark, sin-filled world where everything and everyone is tainted by evil, where every single person will die, and where difficulty will mark our days until we meet that same end. Instead, we have the almighty God of the universe, the God who spoke all things into being, working in our lives to show the tremendous power of our Savior Jesus Christ *in us*. That is very good news indeed!

Paul knew the power at work in him. He rejoiced in sufferings. Not in a dark, masochistic way, but because he saw them as the evidence of God's work. He told the Corinthians, "For the sake of Christ, then, I am content with weaknesses, insults, hardships, persecutions, and calamities. For when I am weak, then I am strong" (2 Corinthians 12:10). He was *content* to go through the worst of the worst for the sake of Christ.

There is something attractive about someone who goes through the unbearable and yet remains faithful to Christ. Our bookstores and conference circuits are filled with those who endure great difficulty to the glory and honor of Christ. These saints bear witness to God's power over difficulties.

Why is it that we are inspired when we read someone else's testimony of God's work through difficulties but then feel resentful when we have the opportunity to live it in our own stories? We read these stories in amazement and whisper, "I want to have faith like that!" yet shy away from mere hints of discomfort.

I want to face my difficult circumstances as one with full confidence in God's sovereign plan, content that today, whatever I face, I am right where God wants me. But I struggle. I live in the tension of faith and fear, hope and heartache, disappointment and dependence. Please know that I am writing this for myself as well as you. I do not sit on a mountaintop bestowing my experience from on high. I share with you as one who is trudging along the same difficult journey of life.

As we resolve in our minds to journey toward contentment, we must hold fast to these truths about our circumstances:

- Everyone faces difficult circumstances. Being a Christian does not make you immune.
- Every circumstance you face is an opportunity. An opportunity to grow, to see God work, to experience God's presence, and to show God's power to others.
- God is with you no matter what you face. We have the privilege of relationship with the King of the universe. We have the Holy Spirit dwelling within us. We have Christ dwelling in our hearts through faith. We have promises of His divine intercession, presence, guidance, and protection.
- We are on a journey toward a glorious eternity. This part of the journey is difficult. That destination is beyond amazing. This is temporary. That is lasting. There is nothing in this journey that ruins that destination.
- In whatever we face, we can be certain that God has sent it, allowed it, or will use it according to His plan. I am not a theologian with degrees in "How God Works," so I won't go into the debate of what He causes or doesn't cause. That is not my department. As His

33

child, I trust that if it is in my life, He is sovereign over it.

I am a very visual person, so I appreciate the metaphors of the Bible. My favorite is the Shepherd/sheep picture of following Christ. I especially like it because I find sheep to be highly relatable. I like the imagery of the strong, capable Shepherd holding a helpless little lamb. In my mind, I am one of those fluffy white sheep with the black face and legs called Valais Blacknose sheep (often called the "world's cutest sheep"). Like I said, I am very visual.

If I am a sheep, following the Shepherd closely, I need not concern myself with the route He chooses to take. I can trust His care completely. I can trust this Shepherd, who laid down His life for me. I can trust His voice. I can trust His protection. He never gets lost, takes the wrong road, or leaves me to the predators. He is *good*.

So why does this Good Shepherd lead me—and you—through difficulties? Why can't He always pick the flat, easy path with plenty of lush, green, tasty food, and fresh, gentle streams? The path without the stones that hurt our feet?

Scripture gives us some clues as to what God is doing when we face difficult circumstances. Please know I am not attempting to explain what God is doing in your particular circumstance. Only God knows. And He may or may not choose to reveal that. Sometimes, with the benefit of maturity or hindsight, when we look back from a great distance, some things make more sense. I am firmly convinced we will not understand most of our life circumstances until we have arrived at our eternal destination. I offer the following encouragements to remind us that as we journey toward contentment, we can develop peace *in difficulties* because we can know that our Savior is doing good for us, even when the situations we face don't appear good to our human eyes.

The following chapters are offered as hope to see how your good and gracious Shepherd may be at work in your life through your circumstances. *Do not* (I repeat strongly, *do not*) use what follows to explain someone else's circumstances. You know so little of what God is doing in your life, how could you possibly know what He is doing in another's? One of the greatest mistakes we make as a church is to turn the promises of God into platitudes or weapons to wield against the hurting. Just love them, and let God be the one to teach them what He is doing.

Circumstances Discipline Us

I think, like many people, when I heard that God disciplines His children, I first thought primarily in terms of punishment. As a young believer, when I first read Hebrews 12:6, which teaches that "the Lord disciplines the one he loves, and chastises every son whom he receives," my initial thoughts went to a child who breaks the rules and must be punished for it.

As a parent of adult children, I see the term *discipline* differently. All day—every day—while our children were growing up, my husband, Erik, and I taught them. We had to remind them daily to brush their teeth, pick up their clothes, wash their dishes, speak kindly, do their chores and schoolwork. Most of the time, these instructions were received well, but occasionally, you would have thought we were torturing them by how they reacted to our guidance. We were mean, unfair, cruel, etc. because we made them do chores.

So, why did we? We knew that one day all four of these precious angels would be living on their own. They would have to be responsible for dishes, laundry, trash, vacuuming, and all the other mundane tasks of running a house. They needed to learn the skills as children so they could perform the skills as adults. We disciplined our children to take care of their homes before they had homes of their own. We instructed our children on how to interact with others, pay bills, pump gas, and be responsible citizens. Certainly, discipline in the negative sense of correcting wrongs entered our overall parenting. Overall, we trained our children to be adults through discipline.

We have all known or heard stories of undisciplined children. They usually turn out to be spoiled, incompetent, self-indulgent brats. People tend to blame the parents of these children for not intervening with discipline. Our gracious heavenly Father will always do better for His children.

If we are to mature into full-grown adult Christians, we must be trained as little-children Christians first. We must learn the skills that will serve us well as mature believers.

Children do not know what is best for them. We don't either, in our flesh. We tend to seek that which is pleasurable more than what is profitable, just as a child prefers candy to vegetables. We need instruction, guidance, training, and discipline to think and do like our Savior would have us.

"For our good, that we may share in his holiness" and that it would "[yield] the peaceful fruit of righteousness"—these are the two results of God's discipline (Hebrews 12:10, 11). You cannot share in His holiness and righteousness without discipline. The writer of Hebrews introduces the topic of God's discipline with the exhortation that we aren't resisting sin like we should. Sin is the opposite of holiness and righteousness. God uses discipline to remove sin from our lives and to teach us the holy way to walk. We are *His* children. Everywhere we go, we represent Him. We need to learn to walk in holiness to represent Him well. When people see our righteousness, they should immediately think, "Oh, she is just like her Dad!" or "His Father trained him well."

There is another sense in which "discipline" can be used, and I think it applies to our life circumstances as well: the sense of *being* a disciplined person. When we are disciplined (controlled, trained, well-behaved), we show that we have been disciplined by God. There are many who are naturally disciplined, whether through upbringing, personality, or life experiences, but this type of disciplined personhood flows from self. In being disciplined by God, our discipline flows from the work of God within us. It is an inward discipline that radiates from a heart indwelt by the Holy Spirit. Our circumstances provide an opportunity to be trained in these disciplines.

We talk about an aimless, struggling young person, who needs an outside force to teach them responsibility, as needing discipline. Joining the military is often a suggested recourse for such an individual. The expectation is that through the regimented training of boot camp and the stern control of a drill instructor, the young person will transform. Certainly, the military *can* teach an individual to conform to a set of community standards.

While there is no spiritual boot camp for new believers, Scripture urges us as new Christians to be trained and become disciplined, to practice the disciplines of the godly life. It is the partnership with the Holy Spirit to learn, apply, follow, and teach the teachings of Jesus. We are disciplined to obey, becoming disciples. We learn His teachings and practice them through the disciplines of the faith: Bible reading, prayer, corporate and private worship, fasting, service, submission, and so on.

Paul uses the metaphor of physical exercise and training in several different letters to illustrate the intentional focus required to train spiritually. We can relate to this metaphor because, like during Greco-Roman times, our culture places a high premium on the athletic lifestyle. Even the most unfit among us know the discipline and effort required to become a successful athlete. We also know the difficulty of starting and maintaining a physical fitness regimen. We know it will require strain, endurance, commitment, and pain. Lots of pain.

Keeping that in mind, Paul says, "Every athlete exercises self-control in all things. They do it to receive a perishable wreath, but we an imperishable. . . . I discipline my body and keep it under control" (1 Corinthians 9:25–27). He reminds Timothy, "train yourself for godliness; for while bodily training is of some value, godliness is of value in every way, as it holds promise for the present life and also for the life to come" (1 Timothy 4:7–8). He also says salvation is "training us to renounce ungodliness and worldly passions, and to live self-controlled, upright, and godly lives in the present age" (Titus 2:12).

Discipline and training do not come naturally—or easily—to me. I really must work at it. In many ways, it goes against how I was made. But there are no qualifiers to these instructions. Paul does not say, "Do this unless you are an Enneagram 9," or "Only type A personalities need to be trained in holiness!" No, these instructions are for all of us. While I may struggle to *be* disciplined, those who are naturally disciplined may bristle under the guidance of the Holy Spirit. They may prefer to decide what their discipline looks like, rather than submit to His plans for training. These commands are in Scripture because we need them, no matter what our natural tendencies may be.

The highlight reels and training montages of today's media lead us to believe that one can be transformed into a super athlete in the length of one song. I have learned in my physical discipline—but even more so my spiritual discipline—that training looks more grueling. Training takes a long time. In fact, we will not achieve our victory until we reach eternity. Our training is meant to be daily, lifelong, and ongoing. It should continually increase in difficulty. We are to grow more disciplined and self-controlled. We are to be characterized by endurance, perseverance, self-control, and steadfastness.

When we reach difficult circumstances, it is an opportunity for us to examine our discipline. God is teaching us, training us, correcting us, or even chastising us in these times. I am not saying that every circumstance is God specifically disciplining us. I am saying that *in* every circumstance is an opportunity *to be* disciplined. God may not have sent the guy in traffic to cut you off, but realizing you reacted in inappropriate anger when you were cut off is an opportunity to repent and pay attention to your tendency to get angry.

In even the most painful, difficult circumstances is the opportunity to be trained by God and to increase our own personal investment in our training.

Our thought process in this matter should never be that of a petulant, spoiled child who blames God for the difficulty, because He wants to discipline us. We should rather seek what training and discipline is offered to us in the difficulty. God's purpose in our lives is to make us like Christ, who learned obedience through what He suffered (Hebrews 5:8), so we, His little brothers and sisters, can learn obedience through our sufferings. Jesus suffered on behalf of our sins, so we must suffer on our own behalf, to learn to resist sin and to love holiness.

SIX

Circumstances Expose Sin

BOTHERSOME CIRCUMSTANCES HAVE the tendency to bring out our best . . . or worst. Usually, the worst. God lovingly, graciously, tenderly uses these uphill climbs and rocky paths to expose our sin.

Sin is anything we say, do, or think that does not glorify God. Anything objectionable to God. Furthermore, Romans 14:23 teaches "whatever does not proceed from faith is sin."

I do not like to look at my own sin. I prefer to walk blindly along, seeing myself as basically having it all together. I see myself as a good, godly person. But in reality, I am selfish, self-seeking, proud, quick to anger, slow to listen, unloving, unmerciful, and unjust. And that is just the tip of the iceberg.

When I face unpleasant times, my ugly nature comes out. The same is probably true for you. I immediately think of me, myself, and I. I act, not in faith, but in willfulness. I have pet idols such as safety, security, my routine, my plans, my money, and my free time, all of which get exposed in trials. God has used difficult times to show me where I lack faith, where I am clinging to worthless idols, how selfish I still am, how little I care about His glory. Graciously, little by little, God shines the light on these private places of my heart to expose them to His truth and light. Softly, tenderly, the Lord says, "Now that I have shown you that sin, let's address it."

Since I began pursuing contentment, I have begun to be more aware of my own discontent. I see my grumbling, complaining, whining when times are tough. Through seasons of difficulty, God has used His Word to reveal that grumbling against the Lord is sin. How very, very much grumbling I have done.

"We must not put Christ to the test, as some of them did and were destroyed by serpents, nor grumble, as some of them did and were destroyed by the Destroyer" (1 Corinthians 10:9–10). Paul was speaking of the Israelites: God's chosen people, recently redeemed from slavery in Egypt. These people were not even out of Egypt five minutes before they started grumbling and complaining. In fact, before they had crossed the Red Sea, they were accusing Moses of taking them into the desert to die. Three days after crossing the Red Sea, they were grumbling again. In fact, the entire forty-year wilderness trek was marked by grumbling. In Deuteronomy 1:27, they even murmured in their tents: "Because the Lord hated us he has brought us out of the land of Egypt."

We would like to think we are not like the Israelites. But we are. They had miraculous delivery from slavery. So do we. They had the Passover. We have the true Passover Lamb. They had redemption of their lives. We have the redemption of our souls. They had miracle after miracle, provision after provision. Yet new challenges brought new grumblings.

Do you forget the work of God in your life easily? Do you face a new trial or difficulty and suddenly forget all the previous difficulties God has brought you through? Have you ever questioned if God actually loves you because of your circumstances?

Yep, me too.

Jude, addressing the issue of ungodly people who had crept *into the church*, brings a prophecy of Enoch, the man who walked with God and was no more because God took him (Genesis 5:21–24). Enoch tells us the fate of the ungodly: judgment and conviction. Jude is clear that the punishment awaiting these false teachers is punishment, a punishment of eternal fire (Jude 1:7).

Enoch speaks of these ungodly people, who practice deeds of ungodliness in ungodly ways (Jude 1:15). These are certainly not people we want to emulate. Yet we join in with them whenever we grumble and complain. Jude 1:15 condemns the harsh things these ungodly sinners have spoken "against him," meaning against God. These ungodly men have spoken harshly against God. Hard. Rough. Violent. Offensive. Intolerable.

When we complain and grumble, this is how we speak against God. We accuse Him of things that are not true, accusing Him of betraying His character and His Word, of breaking His promises. We allow feelings about our circumstances to become our feelings toward God. We allow emotions to overshadow truth. This is ungodliness at its worse.

And it is in me! His beloved child! If I am seeking to be content, complaining is my enemy. Grumbling is my foe! I cannot be a grumbler and be content.

Jude calls the grumblers "malcontents" (Jude 1:16). The prefix *mal* means bad, wrongful, ill, or evil.[1] We see this in malady, maleficent, and malignant. It is someone *chronically* discontent and dissatisfied. They are bellyaching, complaining, disgruntled, unhappy, unsatisfied people. Not only do they have an inner disposition toward malcontent, but they also often voice their accusations against God.

Brothers and sisters, this is the reason we must tread carefully when we begin to question God. The line between praying "Why? I want to understand!" and "How dare you!" is paper thin. We slip from earnest pleading to murmuring and complaining.

The querulous nature of the ungodly *should not* define *God's* people. Heaven forbid! If He is trustworthy, who are we to grumble against Him? If He is good, why do we become malcontents when we go through difficult times?

We act on what we believe. One hundred percent of the time. If we say we believe God loves us, wants the best for us as our Good Shepherd, yet we grumble and complain, our actions reveal the truth about what we believe. Discontent reveals we do not believe God is faithful, just, and wise. Whining reveals we do not believe He is the almighty King of the universe who works all things for our good, who will never leave or forsake us. Our querulousness proves we want to rule our own lives. Fretting and fear expose our disbelief in the riches and glory of eternity promised; they reveal our conviction that this life is all we have.

God so graciously reveals these ill-tempered thoughts so we may repent.

I know I have thought things of God I would be ashamed to say aloud. I will not even write them here, lest you be tempted to think them too. I confess my malcontent. As a beloved child, I have spoken ill in my heart of my good, loving, gracious, patient, and wise Father.

Every challenging and difficult circumstance is a fresh opportunity for God to expose our sin, both in our reactions and discontent. Every time we face something we would rather not, we learn a little more of what it means to believe in God. We see a little more of where we lack faith. God's loving exposure of our sin is an opportunity for the Holy Spirit to remove it from our hearts.

SEVEN

Circumstances Prepare Us

WHEN I WAS A CHILD, my dad was a karate instructor. Many unhappy students walked away from their first lesson disappointed they weren't taught how to deliver a death blow, or kick through a board, or do the "crane" move that emblazoned every *Karate Kid* movie poster. New students were disappointed to learn he taught according to the traditional method of stances, punches, kicks, and katas. Slow and steady. One skill building on the next in repetition and prescribed succession.

What faithful students learned—and what we learn through our difficulties—is that early lessons prepare you for something down the road. Much of early karate training is building strength, endurance, and muscle memory.

A novice often cannot see the result of the initial seasons of preparation.

When we go through our times of difficulties, God may be preparing us for something specific in the future. And if not, He is still shaping us for who *we* are meant to be in the future. God may teach us a skill we will use down the road. He may guide us into reaching for the Word and prayer as a reflex. He may give us a quote,

Bible verse, worship song, or travel companion that fills our hearts with courage for the present trial and becomes a source of hope in future challenges. He strengthens our muscles through repeated usage of trust, endurance, perseverance, steadfastness, and commitment. Still, other times, He teaches us something so meaningful and personal in our darkest times and then places someone in our path later who needs that same truth in their darkest time.

In the book of Genesis, we see Joseph was given the skill to interpret dreams, but when he practiced with his own dreams in the presence of his brothers, it led to several major difficult circumstances, including a murder plot, slavery, and wrongful imprisonment. God gave him the opportunity to interpret the dreams of two very frightened fellow prisoners, using a skill that had been dormant for a few chapters of the story. It took two full years for this skill to be used again, this time with Pharaoh. God then used Joseph's other skills—management, organization, and foresight—to save Egypt and his own family. Joseph practiced these skills as a slave and as a prisoner.

Joseph gave God the glory for how He worked through all these circumstances when he told his brothers (who were the earthly cause for his years of suffering), "As for you, you meant evil against me, but God meant it for good, to bring it about that many people should be kept alive, as they are today" (Genesis 50:20). Joseph did not make light of his circumstances. His brothers meant it for evil. He calls that out. He was hurt. He was probably angry at times. When you read the story of how he revealed himself to his brothers, this was a man of bitter weeping.

And yet, he saw how God had worked through his trials to prepare, strengthen, and train him. He was sitting as second in command of Egypt, with power over everything, save Pharaoh himself, because God had shaped, gifted, equipped, and prepared him (Acts 7:9–10). He knew that even the difficulties were part of God's plan to save his brothers, which ultimately means Judah was saved so our Savior could be born of his line (Genesis 45:5–8; 50:19–20).

Like Joseph, Paul was a man uniquely prepared for the tasks God gave him. It is hard to imagine that as a bright, studious young Jew, he had any idea God would use his training and education in the ways He did. Paul would have left home at a young age when he became a student of Gamaliel. This would have been difficult, rigorous training. According to Acts 22:3, Paul calls this the "strict manner of the law of our fathers." He spent his life dedicated to the heavy yoke of the Pharisees, with its demands of legalistic right-eousness.

When Paul came to Christ, his entire life was turned upside down. The Christians were not waiting eagerly in the wings to embrace him as a brother, this Christian-killer turned Christian. I don't think we can underestimate the difficulty Paul faced in the early years of his faith in Christ. God used those years of isolation to be years of study. God used Barnabas to mentor Paul, which set the pattern for how Paul would later mentor other young believers like Silas, Timothy, and Titus. God prepared Paul through the difficulties of his training as a Pharisee to refute the claims of the Judaizers.

God used Paul's difficult circumstances to propel him forward. God used Paul's difficult circumstances to make him a proficient letter writer and defender of the faith. God used the difficult circumstances of the churches Paul loved and cared for to bring us most of our New Testament. Paul was uniquely equipped to write these letters because of his decades-long preparation through difficult circumstances.

Since we have no insight into our futures, how foolish we are to bristle under our current circumstances. Without the benefit of omniscience, we don't know what these circumstances offer us in preparation for the future. We don't know what we don't know. When we accept our current difficulties as preparation for future ministry and responsibilities, the challenges we face become teachers instead of burdens.

If you are going to be used of God, He will use difficult circum-stances to train and prepare you. We might think, "Well, I just won't be used by God then!" Beloved reader, that will not spare you from difficulty. It will not spare you from sorrow and trials. It will only waste the difficult circumstances. How good and gracious our King is to redeem the hardships common to all mankind and transform them into instruments of His training! You are God's workmanship, handcrafted to do good works. God prepared these good works in advance for you! Why would you choose to miss out on that partnership?

EIGHT

Circumstances Teach Us Endurance and Steadfastness

BECAUSE OF HOW God made me, I struggle with words like endurance and steadfastness. I prefer soft words like connection, relationship, closeness, beauty. I pull away from words like schedule, completion, deadline, perseverance, and results.

Though I embrace my nature and celebrate how God made me, I also know that this is an area where I need to grow and develop. Notice I didn't use words like "overcome" and "achieve" or even "strive!"

I am a work in progress.

By nature I am not an enduring person in many regards. I am a quitter. Often, it is not that I quit per se, but *quit* does seem like a hard word to my soft ears. I lose interest. I get distracted. I move on to the next big idea. I drift or flutter to the next shiny thing.

Because endurance and steadfastness are character traits of God's people, I am working with the Holy Spirit's guidance to change this about my own character.

God wants us to learn endurance. Not simply earthly, complete-what-you-started endurance, but fight-the-good-fight, finish-the-race endurance.

And hardship is how we learn.

To endure is to continue in the same state; to remain firm under suffering or misfortune without yielding; to undergo (as a hardship) especially without giving in. To endure builds endurance, the ability to withstand hardship, adversity, or stress. We see this illustrated in physical training. No one with a lick of sense would attempt an Iron Man triathlon, marathon, or powerlifting competition when their only previous exercise was lifting a remote and a bag of potato chips. It is through systematic training and endurance building that one prepares for an athletic competition. You push yourself further each time you train, thus enduring more and more.

The writer of Hebrews teaches, "You have need of endurance, so that when you have done the will of God, you may receive what is promised" (Hebrews 10:36). And as Peter instructs, "But if when you do good and suffer for it you endure, this is a gracious thing in the sight of God. For to this you have been called, because Christ also suffered for you, leaving you an example, so that you might follow in his steps" (1 Peter 2:20–21).

To be steadfast is to be "firmly fixed in place: immovable; not subject to change; firm in belief, determination, or adherence; loyal, faithful."[1]

How do you know if something is immovable? You try to move it! Our difficult circumstances will try to move us—to move us away from our faith, to alter our course. Our circumstances test our belief. Our trials test our loyalty and faithfulness.

James writes, "Count it all joy, my brothers, when you meet trials of various kinds, for you know that the testing of your faith produces steadfastness. And let steadfastness have its full effect, that you may be perfect and complete, lacking in nothing" (James 1:2–4). The word for steadfastness in this verse can mean cheerful endurance. Yes, cheerful!

Paul teaches in one of his letters, "Therefore, my beloved brothers, be steadfast, immovable, always abounding in the work of the Lord, knowing that in the Lord your labor is not in vain" (1 Corinthians 15:58). He praises God for the "labor of love and steadfastness of hope in our Lord Jesus Christ" of the Thessalonian believers (1 Thessalonians 1:3), and he boasts to other churches of their "steadfastness and faith" in the face of their persecutions and the afflictions they are enduring. Paul tells Timothy to "pursue righteousness, godliness, faith, love, steadfastness, gentleness," and reminds him that he has followed Paul's example of "my teaching, my conduct, my aim in life, my faith, my patience, my love, my steadfastness, my persecutions and sufferings . . ." (1 Timothy 6:11; 2 Timothy 3:10–11). He instructs Titus to teach that "older men are to be sober-minded, dignified, self-controlled, sound in faith, in love, and in steadfastness" (Titus 2:2).

It is the believer who remains steadfast, firm in belief to the end. It is steadfastness that takes the believer to the end, and steadfastness that proves the believer is true. James echoes this: "Behold, we consider those blessed who remained steadfast" (James 5:11).

Peter also gives steadfastness as one goal of the faithful believer, urging his readers to add virtue, knowledge, self-control, steadfastness, godliness, brotherly affection and love to their faith in increasing measure (2 Peter 1:5–7). He says these will "keep you from being ineffective or unfruitful in the knowledge of our Lord Jesus Christ" and keep the believer from falling (2 Peter 1:8–10). These qualities are so important to Peter, he says, "I intend always to remind you of these qualities . . . I think it right, as long as I am in this body, to stir you up by way of reminder" (2 Peter 1:12–13).

I do not want to be ineffective or unfruitful in the knowledge of my Savior! By growing in steadfastness—allowing trials and difficulties to bear that fruit—we are showing our calling and election to be sure (2 Peter 1:10).

The reason our endurance and steadfastness are so important, however, is not what it says about us but what it says about God.

When we endure suffering—especially suffering on account of our faith in Jesus—we glorify *His* suffering as the majestic offering it is! When we remain steadfast through challenging, tragic, difficult, excruciating circumstances, we declare that we have a sure and steadfast anchor for our souls: God who is unchanging, unable to lie, and unable to break His promises; a Savior who has gone as a forerunner and entered the holiest of places on our behalf (Hebrews 6:18–20). We testify that we are the children of the God whose steadfast love and faithfulness guard and protect His people. We demonstrate our belief with our actions and attitudes.

Paul could say, "I have learned to be content in every situation" because he knew the work God was doing in his circumstances (Philippians 4:11). Paul did not just begrudgingly go through difficulty, but said, "We rejoice in our sufferings, knowing that suffering produces endurance, and endurance produces character, and character produces hope, and hope does not put us to shame, because God's love has been poured into our hearts through the Holy Spirit who has been given to us" (Romans 5:3–5).

We are commanded to endure and persevere. We are doing the will of God when we endure. Why? Paul calls God the "God of endurance and encouragement" in Romans 15:5. He reminds us that everything "written in former days was written for our instruction, that through endurance and through the encouragement of the Scriptures, we might have hope" (Romans 15:4). We read in Scriptures the accounts of the faithful who endured so we can be encouraged to endure. We have hope because we know their faithfulness fulfilled the will of God, as ours does as well.

We firmly fix our eyes on Jesus, with confident hope in our salvation. Our hope grows through our faithful endurance.

Biblical hope is not a wish or a dream. It is a guarantee. It is trusting in the unseen with confident expectation. As we go through easy times, our confident expectation gets put more upon ourselves and our ability. Suffering, difficulties, challenges, and hardship put our focus back on the hope we have in Jesus Christ. Paul reminds us of the hope that will not put us to shame for while we were weak, Christ died for us, the ungodly (Romans 5:7–11).

One hundred percent of our hope relies on the love of the Father demonstrated on the cross and the love poured out into our hearts through the Holy Spirit. Suffering teaches us how great the love of the Father is for us. As Paul asks regarding this love, "Who shall separate us from the love of Christ? Shall tribulation, or distress, or persecution, or famine, or nakedness, or danger, or sword?" (Romans 8:35).

Since he had endured these things, Paul could confidently

answer his question: "No, in all these things we are more than conquerors through him who loved us. For I am sure that neither death nor life, nor angels nor rulers, nor things present nor things to come, nor powers, nor height nor depth, nor anything else in all creation, will be able to separate us from the love of God in Christ Jesus our Lord" (Romans 8:37–39).

We like to put "We Are More Than Conquerors" on T-shirts and mugs because it makes us feel like Christian superheroes. However, Paul lists dire circumstances in which we are more than conquerors: tribulation, distress, persecution, famine, nakedness, danger, sword, death, as sheep being slaughtered. The kind of hardships Paul faced. Yet he had confidence in God's ability to keep and guard him. There is a connection here. The more you go through for Christ's sake, the more you endure, the more you persevere, the more hope you have. The more confident expectation you have *because* of the hardships you go through.

NINE

Circumstances Change Our Perspective

I AM ALWAYS fascinated when my eyes see one thing but my brain knows another. I see a planet hanging in the sky as a pin drop of light. Or I see the same planet with the benefit of a high-powered telescope as a grainy image in an eyepiece. Yet I know a planet is huge. Jupiter is more than three hundred times the mass of Earth yet is barely visible to the naked eye.[1] I see the Earth as gigantic, yet it is a small planet. The moon and the sun appear to be the same size in the sky. The radius of the moon is a measly 1,079.6 miles compared to the sun's 432.45 thousand miles![2] Yet they can eclipse each other perfectly from our perspective.

Our brains often have two sets of information to balance: what we see and what we know to be true.

Spiritually, we need to learn the difference between what we see and what is true. We need to gain perspective. Perspective and wisdom go hand in hand. Perspective is viewing matters properly. You need wisdom to see things for what they are. You need to view things properly to know the right thing to do in each situation, which is wisdom.

Through hardships and difficulties, God teaches us wisdom and perspective. God uses our circumstances to shift our focus, to bring us closer to reality. He gives us a heart of wisdom as we seek Him through our shifting perspective.

When you look through a high-powered telescope, you will probably see the image upside down or backward. What you are seeing is a series of refractions and reflections used to focus the light coming off the object. While it looks like you are looking at an object, you are not. It is all lights, lenses, and mirrors. Where the lenses and mirrors are placed determines the magnification. But you still see the image backward.

Our hardships teach us that we see life backward. We see our life through a series of reflections and lenses as well. And to fleshly eyes, it is just a poor image of a distant object. In our flesh, we think that this life—our flesh-and-blood, human existence—is all there is. Our tombstone will have a start date, an end date, and a hyphen in the middle to signify everything that happened in between. When this is our perspective, we live a grasping, striving life seeking to fill up the hyphen part with as much as we can. We live by the motto "Eat, drink, and be merry, for tomorrow you may die." Our perspective fuels our drive to experience, acquire, and achieve.

Through our trials, God teaches us to put this life in proper perspective. *This* life, for the believer, is a drop in the bucket. *That* life, the life promised in Christ, is the life to live for. *That* life is the reality. We live in *this* life as a preparation for the blessed, promised life to come.

When we live with the perspective that this life is the best there is, discontentment grows easily because we want to make the most of this life. Every bump in the road thwarts our desire to live it up while we can. From this perspective, you really are living your "best life" now, so you might as well make it the best you can.

Beloved, the best is yet to come. We cannot grasp with our earthly, fleshly minds this truth because we see with eyes of flesh and interpret what we see incorrectly. As we begin to shift our perspective to eternal matters, worldly wisdom makes less sense. Worldly wisdom is focused on perfecting the experience of this life. A shifted perspective knows that to be foolishness.

Difficulties and hardships reveal how misplaced our hearts are.

Since every challenging circumstance we face is here in *this* life, hardships reveal how focused on the here and now we really are. We can lose every earthly possession, and it has no impact on eternity. We can lose our health and our money. We can lose everything physical, and eternity remains unaffected.

With this perspective, the paradoxes of the faith become clear. When Jesus said, "For whoever would save his life will lose it, but whoever loses his life for my sake will save it," He flipped our normal way of thinking on its head (Luke 9:24). With the perspective of eternity, it is the truth we should live for. He asks, "What does it profit a man if he gains the whole world and loses or forfeits himself?" (Luke 9:25). Worldly wisdom says to gain the world is the only profit there is to a man. If this world is all there is, then that makes sense. But in the paradox of faith, it is to our detriment to gain the world. We lose by gaining. We gain by losing. This truly is the backward image in the telescope of heavenly perspective!

As our perspective shifts, we begin to see the backward way of all earthly wisdom. As James teaches us regarding earthly wisdom, "But if you have bitter jealousy and selfish ambition in your hearts, do not boast and be false to the truth. This is not the wisdom that comes down from above, but is earthly, unspiritual, demonic. For where jealousy and selfish ambition exist, there will be disorder and every vile practice" (James 3:14–16).

Earthly wisdom teaches us to put ourselves first, to be ambitious and accomplish much in our own name. Heavenly wisdom teaches us to put others first, to pursue much in the Lord's name. Godly wisdom is meek and will be shown in good works. "But the wisdom from above is first pure, then peaceable, gentle, open to reason, full of mercy and good fruits, impartial and sincere. And a harvest of righteousness is sown in peace by those who make peace" (James 3:17–18).

Earthly wisdom says, the one with the biggest monument to himself wins. Heavenly wisdom says, "You must be content to suffer, to die, and to be forgotten."[3]

Earthly wisdom says, if it feels good, do it. Heavenly wisdom says, "If anyone would come after me, let him deny himself, take up his cross and follow me" (Matthew 16:24).

Earthly wisdom says safety and comfort are necessities. Godly wisdom says, "He is no fool who gives what he cannot keep to gain what he cannot lose" while running headlong into danger for the sake of the gospel.[4]

Godly wisdom sees the fruit of living according to the flesh and wants to flee from that kind of rotten produce. Godly wisdom sees that the life lived in the flesh bears no fruit worth taking into the Promised Land, but only brings the wrath of God. Godly wisdom wants to have nothing to do with anything that brings wrath. Godly wisdom wants to bear the fruit that can be carried into eternity—both the fruits of making disciples and being a disciple, because those are eternal.

In our flesh, we—individually—are the only one who matters. I am my priority. I am my own master. I am my own servant as well. I serve and indulge myself when the flesh reigns.

When challenges come to those with a fleshly mind, their focus turns ever more to themselves. "Woe is me!" they cry. Trials and hardships are an excuse for further selfishness and self-reliance. They may try harder in their flesh to master their circumstances to their own advantage. They may try harder to control themselves, others, or their situation. They may turn to indulgence or substances to soothe themselves. They may manipulate, isolate, or turn to self-destructive patterns.

But to those of us whose hearts are focused on Christ, trials pull our eyes from self. If wisdom and perspective teach us that eternity is all that matters, the eyes get drawn from our own circumstances to the things of eternity. As we seek the Lord's will for walking in light of an eternal destination, the priorities of that kingdom become our own.

Jesus gave us two signposts for our journey: love God and love our neighbor (Matthew 22:37–39). John 13:34–35 and John 15:12 both record Jesus issuing the command to love one another. In fact, Jesus is clear that this is how people will know we are His disciples. Paul, Peter, James, John, and the writer of Hebrews all reiterate the point that loving one another is mandatory for Christians.

Our difficulties and trials teach us to take our eyes off ourselves and put them where they matter: on God and on others. With the benefit of perspective, every circumstance—good, bad, somewhere in the middle—becomes an opportunity to practice these commands. Paul explains it this way to the Corinthian church:

> [God] comforts us in all our affliction, so that we may be able to comfort those who are in any affliction, with the comfort with which we ourselves are comforted by God. For as we share abundantly in Christ's sufferings, so through Christ we share abundantly in comfort too. If we are afflicted, it is for your comfort and salvation; and if we are comforted, it is for your comfort, which you experience when you patiently endure the same sufferings that we suffer. Our hope for you is unshaken, for we know that as you share in our sufferings, you will also share in our comfort. (2 Corinthians 1:4–7)

Paul calls God the Father "the God of all comfort" (2 Corinthians 1:3). Paul saw that to receive comfort from God was for the purpose of being able to offer comfort to others.

In case you haven't grasped how many trials Paul endured or how extreme his suffering was, here is what he says in the next paragraph: "For we do not want you to be unaware, brothers, of the affliction we experienced in Asia. For we were so utterly burdened beyond our strength that we despaired of life itself. Indeed, we felt that we had received the sentence of death" (2 Corinthians 1:8–9).

If anyone is qualified to teach on the purpose of suffering, Paul is the man! He goes on, "But that was to make us rely not on ourselves but on God who raises the dead. He delivered us from such a deadly peril, and he will deliver us. On him we have set our hope that he will deliver us again" (2 Corinthians 1:9–10).

Paul's focus is on the "God who raises the dead," even facing deadly peril. Paul knew that even if the afflictions he faced resulted in death, he would be raised from the dead. He would ultimately be delivered. He pointed out that God used these circumstances to make him rely on Himself. Do not believe the platitude "God never gives you more than you can handle." That is a bold-faced lie! God will, in fact, give you more than you can bear *so that* you learn to rely on Him. Most of us can handle more than we think we can in our own strength. How do we learn to *rely on Him* if we are never pushed beyond our own capability?

Paul was a man of tremendous perspective. He had a wisdom and insight into the workings of God that makes my brain hurt to try to comprehend. Paul was a wise student under his sufferings. He let them teach him, refine him, and grow him. He let each circumstance refocus his perspective on Christ and others. We can be wise students under our circumstances as well.

TEN

Responding to Your Circumstances
(Part 1)

GOD MAY BE USING your circumstances to teach you discipline, to prepare you, to teach you perseverance, or to change your perspective. This is by no means an exhaustive list. It is not a checklist. It is not an order of events. Our circumstances have much to teach us, but we must be cautious not to think of them as moralistic lessons where once we learn the reason, our difficulties will fade like after the climax of a fairy tale. There will be no "fairy godmother" appearing to sum up our difficulty and tell us the moral of the story. Often, we only see the fruit of the teaching much later.

So far we have looked at what God does in our circumstances. What are *we* supposed to do? What is *our* part?

Get closer to the Shepherd

Like I said before, I think of myself as a little sheep following my Shepherd. I want my little-sheep face right up against His robes. I want to be following so closely I bump into Him if He stops suddenly. I want to be close enough to hear His voice constantly.

But as a sheep, I am prone to wander. Prone to chase butterflies or to stop walking because I am daydreaming. I hear other voices and drift off to follow them and see what they have to say. I look for shortcuts. I look for places to stop and enjoy the view. I get in quarrels with the goats and with other sheep.

I am more prone to wander when my circumstances are good. I am more likely to do my own thing when we are walking through a lush green valley with plenty to eat and no predators in sight, when the breeze gently drifts along with the scent of wildflowers. I am likely to drift along myself. I am likely to find a sunny spot to enjoy the luxury of a peaceful time.

When times are tough, I look to Him more quickly. I seek His help and comfort. I get scared and want His presence. I think it is human—or sheep—nature. It is our nature to think ourselves fully capable in good times but seek refuge when trouble looms.

The goal in seeking contentment is to find the peace of trusting God completely at all times. We must seek Him more fully in the good times. We must draw near to Him, rather than every little whim that floats past, and make Him our sole focus. No longer controlled by our nature, we must seek to listen to the Spirit that dwells within us, listening intently to our Shepherd's voice.

When we stay close to Him during the pleasant circumstances, we are more prepared when the difficult ones come. We do not need to rush to catch up to Him because we have been straggling. By spending time in the lush green valley getting nourished in His Word, we have a greater reserve in leaner times.

As with any relationship, it takes time, investment, and effort to maintain a relationship with the Lord. We start by constantly turning our attention to Him in prayer. We focus our minds on the things of the Lord. We read the Bible, fellowship with other believers, and participate in corporate and private worship.

God's design for your relationship with Him is 24/7, as-you-go, and constant. *While* you live your everyday life. Since He never leaves you, you are always in His presence. He listens to you constantly. The Holy Spirit speaks to you and prays for you. Jesus intercedes for you. He has given you the Word to teach and encourage you.

When we are motivated by the love of our Savior, we cannot

help but *want* to be in His presence. When we think about how much He did—and does—for us, our hearts should be overwhelmed with longing to be as close to Him as possible. Sticking close to Him is an expression of our faith in Him and our desire to be in His presence. It probably will not change our circumstances. But it will change how we *walk through* our circumstances.

Stick close to the herd

You are a sheep. Sheep need other sheep. Period.

You were saved to be a part of the church. You were given the church for your benefit. You were given to the church for its benefit. The church is the good, wonderful, flawed, life-giving bride of Christ.

Too often, we think of the church as a place to which we go rather than a body of which we are a vital part. We are not saved to be attenders and consumers or participants in an organization. We are saved—together—to be the household of God. We are—together—the dwelling place of God (Ephesians 2:19–23). We are—together—"living stones . . . being built up as a spiritual house" (1 Peter 2:5). We are—together—"a chosen race, a royal priesthood, a holy nation, a people for his own possession" (1 Peter 2:9).

We were made for relationships. We were made for community. We are saved to a new kind of coexistence as one beautiful being for His glory. The commands of the New Testament to love, honor, serve, pray, and care for one another are not optional instructions.

When we are in difficult circumstances, we need the flock. We need them to encourage us, to keep us moving forward, to remind us to yield to the Lord.

When we are in good circumstances, we need the flock to keep us focused on the Lord, to redirect us when we start to drift toward self-sufficiency.

In all circumstances, we need the flock to expose our sin. Let's be honest, if we lived in isolation, we would never have our tempers, selfishness, or pride exposed. We could live happily in the self-delusion that we are sinless. Our sin gets exposed through interaction with others. Other people's difficult circumstances reveal a lot of our sin as well. Judgmental spirits, arrogance, and self-righteousness bubble right up to the surface. It is through the closeness of flock living that we learn the areas where we still need the work of the Holy Spirit to cleanse and renew.

We also need the flock in order to practice forgiveness. Just like our sin gets exposed, so does the sin of others. It is going to happen: you will either be sinned against or sin against others. Because we are sinners. Yes, we have been saved and are being transformed into the image of Christ, but we aren't complete yet.

We need the flock for encouragement, accountability, and instruction. We need the flock to have examples to follow, as well as to be an example for others. We need other sheep to remind us how good, gracious, wise, loving, and trustworthy our Shepherd is.

Every circumstance, good or bad, is an opportunity to turn toward the sheep around you. Every situation is an opportunity to live out the commands of Scripture with those closest to you. Pray for a soft heart and open eyes. Pray to look on your fellow sheep with the same compassion your Savior does. Pray He will use you in their lives to be His instrument of growth, healing, and ministry.

Learn to lament

Lamentation is a beautiful, raw, emotional form of prayer we see in Scripture, but it is lacking in our modern churches.

Lament stirs the part of our soul that longs for eternity, that longs for the wholeness and perfection we cannot experience in this world. This part of us knows there is a rightness unattainable in our lives. Yet we still long for it. We are wounded and torn by this world, which amplifies the desire because in eternity nothing that causes pain will exist. It is more than a longing for perfection; it is longing for the way everything will be made right. Even in heaven, while waiting for God's final redemption of mankind, the martyrs cry out, "O Sovereign Lord, holy and true, how long before you will judge and avenge our blood on those who dwell on the earth?" (Revelation 6:10).

When we read Scripture regularly, we are reminded of the faithfulness of God. We are reminded of His trustworthy character; we learn that abounding in steadfast love is how He describes Himself. We regularly see God's people face terrible circumstances and remind themselves of God's character.

The Psalms give us beautiful examples of this heart-wrenching form of prayer. Almost one-third of the Psalms are songs of lament, while several more contain elements of lament.

Lament always contains expressions of both pain and remembrance. We voice our pain. And we remember God's faithfulness. We pour out our hearts and seek His. We may be honest, real, hurt, anxious, and express it in the deepest groans of our hearts. But we must always pivot to the character of God. We must remember His faithfulness, love, and goodness. We must remember He keeps His promises.

When we lament, we remind ourselves in prayer the truths we have learned from His Word. We hold on to His eternal promises. We can express our pain, fear, hurt, anger, confusion, worry, stress, disappointment, grief, misery, anxiety, anguish, exasperation, or weariness. He is a good, gracious, loving God who cares and who listens.

We must turn back to His promises and His character. We must wrestle our hearts back to faith and trust. The Psalms of lament often contain "but" and "yet" when the psalmist shifts his focus from his problem back to the Lord. "But I have trusted in your steadfast love; my heart shall rejoice in your salvation. I will sing to the LORD, because he has dealt bountifully with me" (Psalm 13:5–6). "Yet you are holy, enthroned on the praises of Israel. In you our fathers trusted; they trusted, and you delivered them" (Psalm 22:3–4).

The people of God remember the faithfulness of God and call upon His character in their trials. This isn't like rubbing a genie lamp and, *poof,* your troubles are over; it is realigning your heart to seek God's face in your hardships.

The lament gives voice to our pain and redirects our hearts to rest on the promises we believe in. We believe in God's goodness and mercy in the sunshine and on the easy paths, and we must remind ourselves of them in the rain and the rocky, thorny, uphill paths as well.

God will be as faithful to you as He was to Abraham, Isaac, Jacob, Joseph, Moses, and David. He will be as good to you as He was to Daniel, Hananiah, Mishael, and Azariah. He is as trustworthy as Elijah, Elisha, Obadiah, and Habakkuk found Him to be. He will deal as bountifully with you as He did with Peter, James, John, and Paul.

True lament also guards our hearts against the sin of complaint. We cannot call on His goodness and accuse Him of doing wrong. We cannot declare we believe His ways to be just while accusing Him of being unfair. We can honestly pray, "I believe; help my unbelief!" when we struggle with what we know and our own lack of trust (Mark 9:24). We will struggle with this tension until the resurrection. But lament draws us into deeper relationship where we can lean against the stable promises of Scripture while our knees are weak and our faith is faltering.

Yield to Him

Yielding. Surrendering. Accepting.

There is wisdom and maturity in accepting that your journey is what it is. There is greater wisdom in accepting that God, in His sovereignty, has brought you to this point. If your Savior is leading you, then why resist the path He deems you to take? God has the benefit of omniscience, omnipresence, and omnipotence. You have none of these. God sees not only your story and the path He leads you on but also the path of every person—throughout history—how they are interconnected, where they are headed. We can trust our path to be for our good because we trust God to be good.

If contentment is deep, quiet, trusting peace in God, we must do what we can to master our own reactions. We may have an initial reaction that is mostly reflex or shock. But then we get to decide how to respond. We can decide to fret, worry, be angry, accuse God, and throw a tantrum; or we can decide to quiet our spirit, trust Him, be calm, and accept the situation.

Inner turmoil makes the circumstances worse than they are. When we are untrusting and unyielding, our thoughts are inclined toward "what should be" or "how it is supposed to be" rather than trust and faith. There may be a storm raging outside us, which is upsetting. But in not accepting the storm, a storm rages out of control within you. Our inner dialogue becomes tumultuous. We begin to think, *Why me? Where's God? I can't do this. This isn't fair . . .* , and we forget God's faithfulness. If we accept our circumstances with calmness and faith, there is only one issue to deal with. If we get agitated, there are two.

It is ludicrous to imagine Jesus having a meltdown when He awoke to find the storm raging. Think of your own inner dialogue. Imagine Jesus reacting that way. Mark's Gospel records the disciples' accusation: "Teacher, do you not care that we are perishing?" (Mark 4:38). But Jesus? Calm acceptance. He was the only content person on the boat that night. He did what He needed to do. No freak-out. No tantrum. No worry. He rebuked the disciples for their lack of faith (Mark 4:40).

Jesus accepted his circumstances with contentment. Jesus was completely at peace with God. He had a sure, steady faith in everything. During His earthly ministry Jesus calmly faced temptation, scorn, confrontations, ridicule, pressing crowds, an overtaxed schedule, physical demands, personal loss, and foolish followers—culminating in His betrayal, suffering in the garden, abandonment, crucifixion, and death.

You might be saying, "But He is the Son of God! Of course He could face all that with peace and contentment!"

Beloved, you are a child of God too. You have been adopted as His own. What is true of the Son is true of you. He dwells in your heart through faith (Ephesians 3:17). His Spirit dwells in you (Romans 8:9–11; 1 Corinthians 3:16; 2 Timothy 1:14).

You can do all things through Him who strengthens you. You can accept whatever circumstances in which you find yourself. You can yield your will to the will of the good and gracious Shepherd who leads you. You can be at peace within your heart by trusting God.

Remember God's faithfulness

What was your life like one year ago? I am writing this in December, so that makes it a little easier for me to remember. Of course, Christmas preparations come to mind. Erik and I went on a long road trip to see two of our children and attend a conference. We visited several friends along the way. In all, it was a memorable December.

What about five years, ten years ago?

In our family five years ago, we were starting to send kids to college as well as homeschooling through the high school years. We were experiencing the struggles of a new season. We were getting ready to say, "See you later," to Erik as he went to Korea without the family for a yearlong Air Force assignment. We knew we would move after the year was up, though we didn't know where. I was facing some serious health concerns, with a lot of tests and unanswered questions.

Ten years ago, we were in the thick of homeschooling. We were starting high school for two of the children and middle school for the other two. Erik was deployed to Afghanistan. I was struggling with grief as I mourned the loss of my father to suicide.

As I think about these times, I can remember much of what I was concerned about. I can remember the feelings associated with these struggles.

But as I look back, I can see God's faithfulness. I can see how He worked, how He provided, how He was there.

As we intentionally remember, we can see where God has been good and gracious every step of the way. We can see in easier, pleasant times how He was faithful. We can see in very difficult, hard, rocky places how He was faithful.

As we remember His faithfulness in the past, it serves to encourage us in the present. Could He really have brought us through all He has just to abandon us now? Is that the kind of God we serve? Absolutely not! He is faithful. He is steadfast. He is trustworthy. He is devoted in love to His own.

ELEVEN

Responding to Your Circumstances
(Part 2)

LET'S explore some additional ways we should respond to our circumstances in order to pursue contentment in the Lord.

Intentionally think on eternity

When I was a young Christian, somewhere I picked up the question, "What will this matter to eternity?" I do not know where I heard it or read it. Someone great may have said it. Or my little brain may have come up with it.

Ninety percent of what gets my attention will not matter in eternity. Maybe more than ninety percent. That means I am stressed, worried, bothered, anxious, concerned about things that are not of lasting value. I let my blood pressure get up over nothing.

However, how I respond might. Being kind and gracious to the tow truck driver might give me an opportunity to share Christ with him. Having a loving, relationship-driven parenting response will have an impact on eternity. Yelling at the postal clerk who has no control over my package . . . well, I can't very well turn around and tell her Jesus loves her after that, can I?

Our natural, default perspective is our little kingdom of one. We look first to our own interests. We are primarily concerned with our rule and reign. By intentionally thinking on God's kingdom, not only do we search for our parts in His work, but we are reminded how short and fleeting our time on this planet is.

You were saved to be a part of what God is doing in this world. You were saved for service. You were saved to be a participant in His kingdom.

I love to read missionary stories. I love to read about how God has used His faithful servants. I get goose bumps when I read about a missionary having *that moment* when the language barrier is broken. My jaw drops when I read about a miraculous provision at just the right time. I cry when I read about the death of a martyr and cheer when I read how God uses seemingly insignificant details to accomplish His purposes.

God has chosen me to be a part of what He is doing. My story is just as exciting, jaw-dropping, goose-bump-giving as any of those! I get to be a small player in God's work in this world. It blows my mind to think that I *get* to be a part of God's glorious design for all of history! I am a nobody. But with the kingdom perspective, I have good works prepared in advance for me to do. I am handcrafted by God for those works (Ephesians 2:10).

This should put everything else into perspective. If I am worried and anxious about things that keep me from my part in God's kingdom, I am worrying about the wrong things. If I am unwilling to do my part because of the concerns of my heart, I am sinning. By keeping the perspective of my role in God's work in the forefront of my mind, I keep the concerns of this world in their proper perspective.

God is at work in Uzbekistan and Machu Picchu. God is at work in the Nakasongola District and Novosibirsk. Throw a dart at the map of the world, and exciting, wonderful, marvelous things are happening in the kingdom of God wherever that dart lands.

But God is also at work in your neighborhood. He is doing exciting, wonderful, marvelous things *right where you are*. And you don't have to get a yellow fever shot or renew your passport to be a part of it!

This shift in perspective turns everyday circumstances into opportunities to be His representatives right where He has put us. They turn very difficult circumstances—cancer, job loss, death of a loved one—into opportunities to display our faith in God's faithfulness. As those around us watch how we handle everything that passes our way, pleasant and unpleasant, we demonstrate what we believe. *How* we handle our circumstances is part of the good works God prepared for us to do.

When we become more cognizant of eternity, we are able to minimize the little irritations of normal everyday life; little things look smaller. But we also magnify God. We make His presence bigger in our lives. We make His worth our central focus. When we live with His ongoing work as our priority, we show that nothing of this world is worth more than Him. We show that everything we have in this world pales in comparison to the glory of Him. When we keep His faithfulness and trustworthiness in view, when we trust in Him and rely on Him, we can be content in any and every situation because it truly is His strength we depend on.

Expect hardship

Expecting hardships and trials is not becoming a melancholy pessimist. It is aligning your expectations with Scripture. It is becoming the ultimate realist. Everyone has difficulties. Everyone. Everyone has hardships, trials, shattered dreams, loss, failure, fractured relationships, heartache, and death. Pain taints the entire human existence.

James said, "Count it all joy, my brothers, when you meet trials of various kinds, for you know that the testing of your faith produces steadfastness. And let steadfastness have its full effect, that you may be perfect and complete, lacking in nothing" (James 1:2–4). *When*, not *if*.

When we expect trials and hardships, when we expect to have difficult circumstances, we are prepared to face them as Christ did, trusting God. We may be blindsided by a particular type of trial—

we truly don't know *what* to expect—but we can save ourselves a lot of emotional energy by remembering trials *will* come.

Between discovery of a circumstance and acceptance of it, we have a choice to make. When we do not expect difficulties, usually the reaction is emotional frenzy. We spend our emotional energy in the endless cycles of "could've, would've, should've." If we have not expected difficulty—if we believe that life should be good and perfect and easy—we have a lot to reconcile mentally and emotionally between expectation and reality.

If we expect difficulty, we can invest our emotional energy where we need to—on God. We can turn to Him for strength. We don't waste our time questioning His love and provision. We can skip the emotional turmoil of wondering why we are facing the circumstances and just face the situation. We can spend our energy on prayer and take the steps we need to take with a clearer head.

Christians often express that they feel lied to or betrayed when they face problems in their lives. They feel like they were promised a life of ease and comfort, but faced with difficulties, they are hurt and angry. The problem is, they are not angry at the person who lied to them; they are angry *at God*.

Brothers and sisters, I say this as gently and lovingly as I can: God never promised you ease and a comfortable, trouble-free life. We live in a world marred by sin.

Why do we expect that simply putting our faith in Jesus would negate the difficulties the rest of the world experiences? Wouldn't the world turn to Jesus in droves if nothing bad ever happened to us after that magical moment of salvation? But who would turn to Jesus for Jesus Himself with that kind of benefit awaiting His followers? We would seek the gifts of ease and pleasure He offers, rather than the Giver of righteousness Himself.

We need to create a culture of realistic expectation in our churches. Hard times will come. Trials are common to us all. This allows us to create a community where we lament together. We remind each other in the truth of Scripture about the faithfulness of God. We rejoice together and mourn together. We comfort each other with the comfort we have received. We can take off the masks of false perfection and counterfeit displays of "the good life." We can be real.

We should expect difficulties in our lives and the lives of every person we encounter. But we should also expect joy, delight, wonder, and worship. We should expect the comfort of the Holy Spirit. And comfort from our fellow believers that goes deeper than platitudes. We should expect the miracle of God's grace and goodness to be at work in our difficulties and the difficulties of others.

Don't compare

We cannot compare our burdens with anyone else's because we do not have the whole story. You may look at someone's life and see what appears to be a great life. You do not know where they have been, what they have previously encountered, what is currently going on, or even what they will face in the future. All you see— from the outside looking in—is a curated view of their lives. Someone who looks like they are walking an easy path might be bearing a burden they never let anyone see.

Comparison is the thief of contentment. We can easily slip into covetousness when we start comparing journeys. We can begin to covet another's life because it seems better than what we have.

We can also slip into insensitivity when we compare how another walks their path. We may judge how they carry their burdens. We can be heartless and cruel with the way we comfort or our failure to comfort. We may offer trite or glib sayings to brush off the pain of a suffering soul. We may tell them what we would do if we were walking that path instead of our own. We may mean well, but we don't always do well.

Sometimes, being a part of the body is difficult. It is hard to rejoice with someone when you are hurting, especially when you are hurting over the same type of circumstance that they are rejoicing in. It is hard to celebrate with them when you long to walk a path of joy that eludes you. But this is the call God has given us—to "rejoice with those who rejoice, weep with those who weep" (Romans 12:15). It isn't easy to set aside your joy for a time to comfort someone in pain. It is not easy to celebrate while tears sting your eyes.

Many in our lives carry enormous burdens but can still say, like Paul, "I have learned in whatever situation I am in to be content" (Philippians 4:11). You can too. The goodness of God is drawing us to be at peace with Him no matter what we face. He is trustworthy, and that is the source of contentment.

I realized as I began studying contentment in circumstances that I do not always trust God. As I examined my own thoughts and feelings when I face difficulty, I realized I have often created a false dilemma: either God is not sovereign or God does not care. I realized my thoughts malign the character of God. God is *always* the sovereign King of the universe. Nothing in my life happens without His consent or orchestration. God also cares for me more than I can know. He loves me as His own child. He has provided salvation for me through the blood of His beloved Son and guaranteed my inheritance with His Holy Spirit, and I somehow think that because of a difficulty in my life, He suddenly stopped caring?

I do not seem to struggle to accept God as the sovereign King when He works things out "just right," when wonderful things happen at just the right time and coincidences line up perfectly on my behalf! I praise Him for that. But when things do not go how I think they should? I feel abandoned by an impotent god of my own imagination.

Jeremiah Burroughs and Thomas Watson both put forth the thesis that acceptance of whatever comes from God's hand into your life is the highest fruit of contentment.[1] Burroughs uses the imagery of accepting the honey from the rock, not just for the honey (the good things that come as a result of trials) but for the rock itself (the difficulties) (Psalm 81:16).[2] This acceptance is to think so highly of God that you believe whatever He deems best for your life is to be the best indeed. Not just because He will work all things for your good through what He deems best, but simply *because* He deemed it best. "In this way, like a honeycomb, it drops sweetness into every condition."[3]

To be content, we must be convinced of God's sovereignty. We must be confident in His ability to decide what is best for our lives. We must humbly lay aside our own reckoning of what "should be," in gracious submission to His will.

The sovereignty of God is one of those topics that many Christians struggle to grasp. If we are honest, we struggle because we do not like the implications. We assert God's power, control, might, ability when we want Him to bend things our way. We know He is almighty God, but only when we expect His might to work on our behalf to create miraculous outcomes that benefit us. What are we asking for when we ask for a healing, for a financial blessing, for something to work out a particular way? Are we not asking God to exert His power over our circumstances in the way only the sovereign King of the universe can? Are we not asking for Him to override a natural physical process in asking for a healing? Are we not asking for Him to override the human will to intervene in the life of a wayward soul? Are we not asking for Him to step in and cancel the laws of physics on our behalf when we pray for protection?

Why do we act like God made a mistake when there is a cancer diagnosis? Or a job loss? Or a weather event? Or whatever else?

We say—almost like a platitude—"God is in control," but when something happens that we do not like, suddenly we are hurt, angry, resentful, belligerent toward God. We are offended that our plans or preferences were not considered when He exercised His control.

Every time the topic of God's sovereignty is discussed, man's will gets brought up, as if the two are diametrically opposed. They are. My will for my life is to do what I want, when I want, how I want. And never to have a single bad thing happen. My will is to live in health, wealth, and happiness forever and ever with all my loved ones equally endowed with the same beautiful, easy, carefree lives. Whenever my will in this matter is violated (and trust me, it has been violated quite often), either I can either accept that my will is opposed to God's will, or I can be angry that my will was not respected.

We never have to learn to submit our will to God's if everything happens as we wish, do we? We never have to learn that His will is best if we only ever have what we want; we never have to learn how reliable He is if we only ever have to rely on ourselves. We would never think of others' pain or suffering if we did not experience our own. It takes no faith to live a life that follows my will and my view of how my life should go. It is trouble that teaches that God is a very present help in time of need; it is in danger that we find Him to be a shield and refuge.

I am not the sovereign God of the universe. I am a weak-willed, feeble-minded, selfish human. I do not know what tomorrow holds, nor the day after. I do not know the end of my story. How could I presume to know what should happen today? I do not even know the impact yesterday will have on tomorrow. I have limited scope and narrow understanding. I have come to realize that most of my discontentment in my circumstances comes from the fact that my circumstances are not what I would have chosen if I were the sovereign ruler of my own life. I multiply that discontent when I accuse God of working His sovereignty for evil in my life.

But God knows all, sees all, understands all. Why do I not trust Him to do best?

We cannot be content until we are unconditionally and thoroughly convinced of God's sovereignty. Every promise of God's loving-kindness toward us, His work on our behalf, His work of goodness in our lives—it all flows from the *capability* of God to work those promises because of His sovereignty. We must accept that we may never know why God caused or allowed certain things; there are questions we may not have answered this side of eternity. We must learn to subjugate our feelings in difficult circumstances to God's truths and the faith those truths inspire. Feelings are petulant, fickle, temperamental, and unreliable. God's truth is sure and steadfast, a reliable refuge. He is unchanging, all-powerful, and good.

Part Three

CONTENTMENT IN CONTEMPLATION

TWELVE

The Guarded Heart and Mind

WE ARE COMPLEX INDIVIDUALS, aren't we? We consist of a physical body, which is a mind-bogglingly intricate system. But we are also heart, mind, soul, and spirit. We are thoughts, feelings, impulses, intuition, memories, dreams. This combination of body and being is what makes us who we are.

The inner part of us, the part that accounts for our being, is where our faith life takes place. It is the essence of who we are. It is the part that departs this world in death and leaves the empty shell of the body behind.

In his writings, Paul addresses this inner part of us frequently. He was firmly convinced that the transformation of this inner part of us is the core of the gospel.

To be content—to have the deep, inner peace that comes from trusting God fully—we must master our minds. Remember, contentment is an intellectual occurrence, a frame of mind as well as a condition of spirit. Paul tells us, "The peace of God, which surpasses all understanding, will guard your hearts and minds in Christ Jesus. . . . practice these things, and the God of peace will be with you" (Philippians 4:7; 9). God promises this peace and guarding as the result of contemplating correctly. In longing for contentment, we are longing for this peace. Paul has spelled it out clearly in this passage: you must master your thoughts. We must pay attention to our hearts and our minds as we walk with the Lord, particularly in seeking contentment.

Heart and Mind

The heart is more than just the organ that pumps blood; it is the seat of who you are. It is the center of your being. Your emotional, moral, intellectual activities stem from your heart. It is the well-spring of your thoughts, actions, and will. You make decisions from the heart. Your heart is the source of your appetites and desires, your motivation. You are given a new heart—a heart of flesh in place of a heart of stone—when you place your faith in Jesus (Ezekiel 11:19). Your heart is circumcised. You, therefore, are to make all your decisions and direct your whole life with this new heart.

The words we translate into *mind* have a wide variety of meanings, including that which makes you a living being, your spirit, or your framework. It is also used much the same way as *heart* is, and many times they are used interchangeably. It also has meanings related to your inner man, your intellect.

In Philippians 4:7, Paul uses the Greek word (transliterated) *noema* for "minds," meaning perception, purpose, intellect, disposition. In Scripture *noema* means mind, thought, and device or designs.[1]

Paul is teaching that God will guard our hearts—the essence of who we are, where we make decisions, where our desires, will, and character dwell, the seat of our soul, the source of our affections, emotions, and passions. He will guard our minds—the part of ourselves where our intellects and thoughts dwell, where Christ has been revealed, and where we purpose to follow Him. The mind is the source of our obedience and devotion.

If our hearts and minds are guarded by God's peace that passes all understanding, contentment cannot help but follow, since it is deep, inner peace that comes from trusting the God of peace.

Rejoice and Be Reasonable

Joy is one of the major themes of the book of Philippians. As Paul writes (he himself was in chains at the time), he reminds the Philippians repeatedly to rejoice. He mentions *rejoice* nine times in seven verses. He uses the word *joy* five times.

Joy is gladness in God. It is cheerfulness, calm delight, a deep-rooted, inspired happiness. Joy is a noun. It is a fruit of the Spirit, which means it is something God intends for you to have in increasing measure. As you increasingly set your affections and attention on the Lord, your gladness in Him will increase. Joy is the natural byproduct of being glad you are the Lord's child and walking in a manner that delights Him.

Rejoice is a verb—an action—meaning to express joy. It is to talk about and proclaim that which has made you joyful. It has the "re" in front of it, which means again, or back, and indicates repetition. To rejoice is expressing joy as a verb, repeating the feeling of joy within you. As we reflect on past moments of joy, the mere act of bringing them back to memory stirs within us the emotional response again. When we give voice to those feelings again, remembering and praising, that is rejoicing.

Paul says, "Rejoice in the Lord always; again I will say, rejoice" (Philippians 4:4). God is the object of our rejoicing. We rejoice in Him. We rejoice to Him. Gladness in God comes from God, and we direct our gladness back to Him as we rejoice.

If you are in Christ, no matter what is happening in your life, you have joy and you can rejoice. You have been given eternal life at the cost of the Son of God. You can rejoice because you walk in the presence of God. You have been given His Holy Spirit to dwell within you, to cheer and to comfort you. We can rejoice always because we always have these promises, we always have God's presence, we always have the Holy Spirit, and Jesus always intercedes for us. Our joy is not based on our constantly changing circumstances; it is based on the never-changing character of God Almighty. It is based on our never-changing status as beloved children.

Rejoicing in the Lord is not our natural state. Paul would not have to issue this repeated command if it were. In fact, the instruction to rejoice in the Lord is found throughout the Scriptures. The Psalms are filled with rejoicing: commands to rejoice, reasons to rejoice, determination to rejoice. The prophets are full of judgment for people who did not rejoice in the Lord. The prophets also speak of future rejoicing when God will have restored His people. Most of the prophets personally rejoiced in the Lord.

Scripture should be our primary source of rejoicing. When we read the Bible daily, we feed our hearts continually with the gladness of God. We learn His character, His ways, and His work in the world. And we can rejoice. When we have a steady intake of God's Word, we set our minds to focus on the work of God around us.

Paul could rejoice while in trials, sufferings, and chains because he was focused on God Himself. This is how James could urge us to count our trials as joy. This is how Peter could urge us to rejoice in sufferings.

This is how we can obey the commands of Scripture to rejoice. We make a conscious decision to focus our attention on God, His character, His marvelous deeds, our eternal hope. We focus on the joy of our salvation, remembering that He removes our sins as far as the East is from the West, that He clothes us in robes of righteousness though all our own righteousness is as filthy rags (Isaiah 61:10). We ponder daily the greatness of the love of God toward us. We turn our thoughts repeatedly to the good things God has done in us, for us, and through us.

And we focus our attention ahead to the greatest time of rejoicing to come: "'Hallelujah! For the Lord our God the Almighty reigns. Let us rejoice and exult and give him the glory, for the marriage of the Lamb has come, and his Bride has made herself ready; it was granted her to clothe herself with fine linen, bright and pure'—for the fine linen is the righteous deeds of the saints" (Revelation 19:6–8).

That is us! John saw us—you and me—at the end of all things, prepared as a bride for the Groom. The church of all history, even those not yet born, gathered for the wedding feast of the Lamb. We will be rejoicing and exulting and giving God praise and glory! This should thrill your heart. If you can think of nothing else in the entire world to rejoice in the Lord, this is plenty! That moment—that glorious, splendid, holy moment—is enough. If you are in Christ, your future is sealed in prophecy and promise. You are God's. You are a part of this spectacular bride of Christ. Every act of right-eousness you partake in becomes a part of the fine linen that will adorn the bride as a gown.

This is jump-for-joy, sing-at-the-top-of-your-lungs good news! *This* is reason to rejoice.

Rejoice.

Always.

Paul urges us to "let [our] reasonableness be known to everyone" (Philippians 4:5). If a character trait is to be known to everyone, it must be present and evident. So, what is reasonableness?

The ESV Bible has a footnote next to reasonableness saying, "or gentleness."

The process of choosing which definition to use for a particular word in an ancient language is a challenge. Our own language has many possible definitions for words. This word, transliterated *epieikes*, means "appropriate, mild, gentle, moderation, reasonable, seeming, suitable, equitable, fair."[2]

This word is a compound word with the root being "be like" or "resemble."

Our gentle, patient, mild, reasonable, gracious, suitable resem-blance to our Savior should be evident to all. As we meditate on the Lord and study His ways, consciously applying the truth of the gospel to ourselves daily, this *reasonableness* will be a natural by-product.

However, Paul is issuing this as a command. There is an instruc-tion to be resolved, to make sure that it is evident when he uses the word *let*. And let's be honest, sometimes that is harder than other times, right? Sometimes people bring out the worst in us—the parts that *least* resemble Jesus—before we even realize what is happening. We must use our thoughts, redeemed by the Lord, to override our natural inclination.

We are to have reputations for being patient, gentle, mild, kind, gracious. As individuals and as churches, we should be known for handling conflict peaceably, for selfless concern for others, for gracious speech, and mild-mannered actions. We should have a sweet reasonableness that attracts nonbelievers.

We use our intellect to study the Scriptures with the aim of seeking Christ's character so we can become Christlike. We use godly wisdom to apply those Scriptures to our lives to eliminate all the negative qualities listed and to allow God to grow the gentleness of Christ in us. We become conscious of the humanity around us, seeking to demonstrate the mild, gentle, peaceable, patient, equitable, moderate nature of Christ to the best of our human ability. Remember, God's goal for us is to become like Christ. We are actively partnering with the work God is already doing when we set our minds toward this aim.

Though different Greek words, the ideas behind kindness, goodness, and gentleness are very similar to the word we have been looking at (Galatians 5:22–23). If you are growing in the Spirit, His fruit will be growing in you. Kindness, goodness, and gentleness are words that are demonstrative; we *show* that we are kind, good, and gentle by how we act toward others. God actively demonstrates His kindness to us (Romans 2:4; 11:22; Ephesians 2:7; Titus 3:4). We are filled with God's goodness, and all that is good is found in Him (Romans 15:14; Ephesians 5:9). Paul called upon the Corinthians to remember the meekness and gentleness of Christ as they listened to his argument (2 Corinthians 10:1). Paul urges meekness to be the attitude with which we walk, an attribute to be put on, and a trait to be pursued (Ephesians 4:2; Colossians 3:12; 1 Timothy 6:11).

What does this have to do with our journey toward contentment? Think on the character of Christ, our ultimate example of contentment, and be like Him. Reasonableness is the outward expression of the inner work God is doing to make you like Christ.

THIRTEEN

Do Not Be Anxious

I WANT you to imagine we are sitting together across a table. Maybe we are at your favorite coffee shop or at my dinner table. Wherever you imagine, I want you to lean in close and listen closely. I would be looking into your eyes as I say this. So, both-ears-open, heart-engaged kind of listening.

There is a difference between being anxious in the sense that Paul is writing about and the medical/mental health condition known as an anxiety disorder. Since Paul is writing this as a command, we must do our best to be obedient. We can never assume, however, that someone with this condition is being disobedient to this command. It is a careful balance between application of Scripture and the limitations of our human frailty. We all have many areas where we live in this tension.

If you have this condition (yes, Christians can have mental health disorders), please know that I write this with love and compassion for your struggles. I know you probably berate yourself and question your faith enough without this chapter adding to that pain. I am not addressing your disorder. I am addressing the willful choice to be anxious . . . to worry.

If you have an anxiety disorder, there is much you can do. I highly encourage you to seek help from a medical professional as well as a licensed Christian counselor or therapist. I encourage you to be honest with your community about your struggles, while you continue to seek the Lord and His holiness.

As we move forward examining this passage, I will use the word *worry*. If you struggle with anxiety, you can apply this passage to your heart and trust the Lord as you navigate this challenge in His grace. The Lord has mercy for you in abundance. Let us lean on Him as we move forward.

Paul writes, "The Lord is at hand; do not be anxious about anything" (Philippians 4:5–6).

Paul gives the "why" first: the Lord is at hand. The Lord is near.

This should be the truth that permeates our heart above every other truth. The Lord is near. The Lord—who loves you, died for you, intercedes for you—is nearby. At hand. His presence is with you always.

He is at hand in another sense, His return. We do not know when that glorious moment will occur. The apostles lived with the expectation that it could happen at any moment. They were eager to see the work completed because they saw His return as imminent. Jesus spoke in His parable often about the unknown time of the arrival of the Master, or Bridegroom. The early disciples took that to heart. We should as well.

The Lord is at hand.

This is a comfort! This is reassurance, not a fear tactic. I have heard many parents remind a disobedient child during the month of December that a certain big guy in a red suit was watching them and wouldn't bring gifts if they didn't shape up. Sadly, many Christians interpret the Lord's presence in this manner. They think God Almighty is following them around looking for an opportunity to smite them for the slightest indiscretion. This couldn't be further from the truth!

God's presence is a watchful, loving, caring presence. He is zealously protective of His own. The Psalmist tells us, "The LORD is near to all who call on him, to all who call on him in truth. He fulfills the desire of those who fear him; he also hears their cry and saves them" (Psalm 145:18–19).

The word Paul uses here that the ESV translates as "anxious" can also be translated as "take thought, careful (as in full of cares or troubled with cares), to look out for self or one's interests, worry." Paul uses this word in the positive sense when he speaks of the church members having care for one another and Timothy's genuine concern for the welfare of the Philippians (1 Corinthians 12:25; Philippians 2:20). He uses it repeatedly in 1 Corinthians 7:32–34 in discussing the benefits of remaining single to devote oneself to the cares of the Lord while the married individual also has the anxieties of pleasing their spouse.

Jesus speaks on worry in His Sermon on the Mount. He issues the commands: "do not be anxious about your life, what you will eat or what you will drink, nor about your body, what you will put on . . . . do not be anxious about tomorrow" (Matthew 6:25–34). He instructs instead, "But seek first the kingdom of God and his righteousness and all these things will be added to you" (Matthew 6:33).

Jesus asserts throughout the Sermon on the Mount that the Father is trustworthy, kind and compassionate, faithful and unchanging. We can trust Him.

But worry reveals our lack of trust.

Worry is the voice of "what if." Since the future in unknown to us, all we have when we think about tomorrow is "what if." When we begin to think about tomorrow, our minds run away with the worst of the possibilities. Have you ever noticed you don't worry about good things? What if I get promoted at work because my boss thinks highly of me? What if we celebrate our seventy-fifth wedding anniversary and die happily in our sleep? What if my children love the Lord and walk faithfully in His ways? No, our runaway thoughts are usually worst-case scenarios.

I encourage you—this one time—to follow your worries to the end. Keep asking, "And then what?" Do you get to a single end of the line and find that God is not there? I will be straight with you, if you believe otherwise, you do not believe God. His Word is emphatic: He "will never leave you nor forsake you" (Hebrews 13:5). Do you actually trust God never to leave you nor forsake you? Make a list of every worry. Think about each and every one of them. If they come true, is God still God? Is He still faithful? Is He still caring for you? Is He still able to save your soul and deliver you to heaven?

If you get to the end of the line of worrying and find yourself thinking, "If this happens, I can't trust God . . . or won't love Him . . . or won't worship Him," you have uncovered an idol. You have found something that is more important to you than God Himself. This is where your heart is, not in Him. In God's grace, He is revealing this to you for repentance. He is showing you what you have put above Him so you may put it at His feet and place Him above everything else.

When we worry, we stir up our emotions. We actually feel the feelings of distress, anger, fear, loss, etc. we would experience if we went through the event (though probably to a lesser degree since we are imagining). We can also have physiological reactions, such as raised blood pressure, to imagined events.

But what if God never intends for me to go through the things I imagine?

I have put myself through an experience emotionally that God Himself did not ordain. I feel emotions of loss and heartache that were not His plan for my life.

And what if I do go through the event?

Well, now I have gone through it twice (or however many times I have imagined it, plus the one real one). Am I any better prepared for having experienced it emotionally in advance? Absolutely not. In fact, all I have done is taken the pain of this future event and brought it into the present. I took the emotions from one season and burdened another season with them.

We use the idiom "We will cross that bridge when we get to it" to say, "Don't worry about that now; we will figure it out when we get to it." When we worry, we cross bridges that we might not ever come to.

I have heard this reasoning: "I am not worrying; I am preparing myself." Unless you are preparing with more diligent reading of Scriptures, prayer, fasting, and generosity, you are lying to yourself. Jesus tells us the only true preparations are storing up treasures in heaven (Matthew 6:20). Investing emotional energy and earthly resources in the direction of your worry is foolishness. As foolish as birds building barns and lilies turning into weavers.

Jesus asked, "And which of you by being anxious can add a single hour to his span of life?" (Matthew 6:27). Of course, this is rhetorical. No one can. It has been proven that through medical studies that anxiety and worry have negative health effects, so you are possibly taking away from your life span. But you are also taking away hours of *living* by worrying. Pacing the floor, studying the stock market, reading health journals, or whatever frantic activity you turn to when you start worrying is not the practice of storing up your treasures in heaven. It is fruitless work, unworthy of a child of the King.

When we are distracted with worry, we are not directing our thoughts toward kingdom purposes. Jesus used the word *anxious* when addressing Martha: "Martha, Martha, you are anxious and troubled about many things, but one thing is necessary. Mary has chosen the good portion, which will not be taken away from her" (Luke 10:41–42).

Mary was focused on the Lord at hand. And nothing else. Martha was focused on everything else and missed the Lord.

We have a choice to make in our thinking. We get to tell our thoughts what they can dwell upon. Yes, thoughts will come into our heads that will stir up what-ifs. But we don't have to entertain them. Charles Spurgeon said, "We cannot help the birds flying over our heads; but we may keep them from building their nests in our hair."[1] You have been given tremendous power over your mind through the power of the Holy Spirit.

The answer to "what if" must be "even if." Every fear you have, everything you worry about can be answered with the "even ifs" of Scripture. Even if, God is faithful. Even if, God is Sovereign. Even if, God loves me. Even if, I have a guaranteed inheritance awaiting me. Even if, He is good. Even if, I will praise Him. For every worry that comes into your head, rather than dwell on and imagine all the horrible possibilities, answer it with "Even if this happens, I will trust God because He is good, He loves me, and He is going to be near."

Habakkuk is our model for this. Habakkuk was told in detail what awaited the people in a coming invasion. He knew the future —and it was scary—and he was terrified. He said, "I hear, and my body trembles; my lips quiver at the sound; rottenness enters into my bones; my legs tremble beneath me" (Habakkuk 3:16). He was literally shaking in his sandals! Habakkuk turns his heart to God and says, "Though [even if] the fig tree should not blossom, nor fruit be on the vines, the produce of the olive fail and the fields yield no food, the flock be cut off from the fold and there be no herd in the stalls, yet I will rejoice in the LORD; I will take joy in the God of my salvation. GOD, the Lord, is my strength; he makes my feet like the deer's; he makes me tread on my high places" (Habakkuk 3:17–19). Even if the worst of the worst happens. Even if I have nothing left. Even if everything is violently destroyed. Even if . . . I will rejoice in the Lord. Even if, I will take joy in God and praise His name.

How sad that we easily forsake pursuing contentment because we worry about the possibilities the future may hold. Our peace with God is too important to sacrifice for imagined events. Redirect your thoughts to God's trustworthiness.

The fruit of the Spirit that correlates to not being anxious is peace. It is a tranquil state of soul that rests in our salvation and trust in our God's loving care. Peace is being untroubled in your heart. Jesus said to his followers, after promising them the Holy Spirit, the Helper, "Peace I leave with you; my peace I give to you. Not as the world gives do I give to you. Let not your hearts be troubled, neither let them be afraid" (John 14:26–27). Jesus says, "Let not your hearts be troubled" twice in this chapter. He really wants us to get this. We *let* our hearts get troubled, and His peace is the solution as we believe in Him and believe Him to keep His word.

FOURTEEN

But Pray

IF TWO PLUS decades of ministry have taught me anything, it is that Christians tend to get uncomfortable with the topic of prayer. I have watched Christians cringe, disengage in Bible study or conversation, and abruptly change the subject when prayer gets brought up. This might be you. The topic of prayer might make you uncomfortable. Read this chapter even if you don't think prayer is for you.

I love talking to children. Love it! In most cases, I would rather talk to children than adults. If I attend an event and children are present, you will probably find me deep in conversation with the younger crowd.

When you start talking to a child and they see you are genuinely interested, they will talk forever. If you get down on their level and make eye contact, you will watch them open up. And children ask amazing questions. I have never had an adult ask me, "What is your favorite funny face to make?" or "Can you run faster than a T. rex?" They see the world through the lens of possibility. They are untainted by cynicism. In their innocence, they do not filter or self-edit. They just talk.

We have a loving Father who is supremely interested in us. He has gotten down on our level and said, "My child, talk to me."

And we say, "Pray? Oh no, I can't do that. I don't know what to say. I don't know how. Prayer makes me uncomfortable. That's for more mature Christians. That's for those in ministry."

Why does prayer make us so uncomfortable? Why do we get antsy when a prayer takes a little long during a service? Why do prayer meetings record the lowest attendance at most churches? Why do we all look away when a leader asks for a volunteer to pray?

Our Father has given prayer as a gift. Stop and think about it. The almighty God, the Maker of heaven and Earth, the Holy One, the One enthroned in heaven has asked you to talk to Him. This God, this glorious, amazing-beyond-all-words God wants *you* to have conversations with *Him*. Amazing!

Maybe you recognize the enormity of God, and that is why you are afraid to talk to Him. I mean, He is the almighty God after all.

We should be like beloved little children telling our wonderful Daddy everything on our hearts. He wants to hear it. He wants us to talk to Him. He wants us to pour out everything.

Paul wrote, "In everything by prayer and supplication with thanksgiving let your requests be made known to God" (Philippians 4:6).

The "but" immediately follows and stands in contrast to "do not be anxious about anything." Paul is telling us these are opposites; one is to be stopped and one is to be practiced. Paul employs this technique throughout his letters. He gives a command, usually in the form of "stop doing what comes naturally," and follows with "but do this," which is only possible through the work of the Holy Spirit and careful attention to obedience. He tells the Romans not to be conformed to the pattern of this world but be transformed by the renewing of their minds (Romans 12:2). This means being anxious falls under the category of the *old me*, while "but in everything pray" is a part of the *new me*.

"In everything." Paul isn't being hyperbolic when he says this. He really does mean *in everything*. In various letters, Paul also encourages Christ followers to pray without ceasing, be constant in prayer, continue steadfastly in prayer, and to pray at all times in the Spirit (1 Thessalonians 5:17; Romans 12:12; Colossians 4:2; Ephesians 6:18).

Every thought we have can—and should—be directed toward God in prayer. To pray in everything, we are turning the constant chatter of our minds into purposeful communication.

You may be thinking, "If God already knows everything, why do I need to talk to Him about it?" The reason: love. Plain and simple. We love the Lord, but the Lord *loves* us. He loves us beyond our wildest, biggest, most extravagant imagining. He loves us so deeply, so thoroughly, so purely, our minds cannot comprehend it. Paul prayed for the Ephesians to be strengthened to comprehend the breadth, length, height, and depth of the love of Christ, which surpasses knowledge! (Ephesians 3:18–19). We talk to God because He cares for us.

My two-year-old nephew was delighted to show me his crayons and tell me each of the colors. He showed me the black (or "back," as he said it) one had been broken. He tried to put the two pieces back together to demonstrate how it was whole before he broke it. Do I already know the crayon colors? Of course. Could I say the names of the colors better than he could? Of course. Could I tell how the black crayon pieces were once one whole crayon? Absolutely. I even know how crayons get made, how the wax can be melted, and how to combine the colors to make new colors. My knowledge is greater than his. But it was a joy to listen to him, in his tiny toddler voice, with mispronunciations and errors, tell me about his life in that moment. Because I love him. Because he came to me in relationship to share it with me.

On a much larger, grander scale, God wants us to come to Him. He wants us to bring our equivalent of a box of crayons and tell Him all about them. He already knows everything. We are not revealing any new information to Him. He just wants us to know He loves us, and He wants us to love Him in return.

By praying always and about everything, we are constantly reminding ourselves of His ever-present being. He is at hand. He is always listening. He hears our every thought, every whisper of our soul. He reminds us we have nothing to be anxious about because His loving-kindness guards us.

When we pray about anything and everything, we are demonstrating that we believe His faithfulness. But more than that, we are growing our own love and faithfulness toward Him. When I spend more time talking to God, I want to talk to Him about His things. I want less "stuff" in the way. I find my heart growing warmer to His will and His ways. I find my affections warmer as well. Did you recognize love and faithfulness as fruit of the Spirit? As we dedicate ourselves to be steadfast in prayer, to be constant in our affections toward the Lord, the Holy Spirit works in us to grow His fruit.

As we turn toward God in love, He also grows our love for others. Paul urges his readers to offer "supplication." This can be a petition to God on our behalf or on the behalf of others. Paul tells the Ephesians to pray with "supplication for all the saints" (Ephesians 6:18). As I spend more time talking to God, I find myself thinking of myself less and others more. I am more aware of others' needs. I begin to see others with the eyes of Jesus. I want others to experience the love of God more and more deeply. I want them to rely on His faithfulness.

As you begin to grow in praying without ceasing, it is a valuable discipline to set aside time in your schedule for dedicated prayer.

Think about your best human relationships. Maybe your marriage or a friendship. Think about when your relationship has been the most fulfilling. I am guessing you had regular, dedicated time together. Our relationship with God is no different. It thrives when we invest regular times with Him. This isn't about adding something to your schedule just to check a box or feel like you deserve a spiritual gold star. This is about connecting. When we set aside time in our busy lives for someone, we communicate to them how highly we value them. How much more should we take the time to invest in our relationship with the One who loves us most of all?

Yes, we are all busy. We all have demanding schedules. And wandering minds. And distractions. And interruptions. And loud homes. Or whatever reason you just thought of. You carve out time for friends, right? You can find time for a girls' night out or a family vacation? You can go on a date with your spouse? You can talk on the phone to your friends? You have time to pray.

You are a unique individual who needs to relate to God as you. You need to figure out what will work best in your schedule, your body rhythm, your personality, your temperament, and even your season of life. Anyone who tells you the only "right" way to pray is to get up at five a.m. and lock yourself in a closet for an hour is wrong. You may pray best in a closet. You may pray best while walking or in a church. You may connect to God at five a.m. or three p.m. Try different times, places, postures, or methods. Use a book or a journal; follow a guide or just share your heart.

But pray. In everything. At all times. Without ceasing. Become faithful in prayer.

FIFTEEN

With Thanksgiving

PAUL WAS ONE THANKFUL GUY. Paul wrote thirteen books of the New Testament, and in *eleven* of his letters, he gives thanks for the recipient, teaches on thankfulness, bursts out in thankful praise, or commands thankfulness in his readers.

Thankfulness was a big deal to Paul. He kept before him the facts of who he was before Christ, what Christ had done, and what God was doing through him. He knew that the love of God had intervened in his life and rescued him from destruction. He knew he had been going zealously in the wrong direction. He remembered his moment of salvation—and what a moment it was!—and knew that Jesus had called him out of death and darkness into life and light. He had a profound sense of "I do not deserve this," which bubbled over into tremendous thankfulness.

Our thankfulness has the same source. If you are in Christ, thankfulness should be a primary character trait. You have been made alive. You have been rescued from slavery to sin. You have been given eternal life. If we turn our minds constantly to who we were, what Christ did, and what God is doing through us, our thankfulness will come as easily as Paul's.

If you are not thankful, start examining your heart. Do you

understand the totality of your own sin nature before Christ? Do you understand how utterly repulsive your sin was—and still is—to God? How great His love must be to remove your sin at the cost of His only Son? Do you understand how much your Savior suffered on your behalf? He not only endured the most painful death (our word *excruciating* comes from the word for crucifixion), but He *became* sin so you could become righteousness. He became the thing that God hates out of love for you. God, incarnate, Word become flesh, became that which God hates. For you.

When we remind ourselves of what God has done in our lives, we grow in our thankfulness.

Paul says, "In everything by prayer and supplication *with thanksgiving* let your requests be made known to God" (Philippians 4:6, emphasis added).

In Ephesians 5:20, within a longer set of instructions, Paul writes, "giving thanks always and for everything to God the Father in the name of our Lord Jesus Christ." Earlier in the same chapter, he cautions that filthiness, foolish talk, and crude joking are not fitting for believers, but instead there should be thanksgiving (Ephesians 5:4).

In Colossians, he gives five separate instructions on thankfulness. He ties thankfulness to the church's unity as a body, the way they should speak to each other, and his instructions to do everything in the name of the Lord Jesus. He issues a command similar to our focal verse, "Continue steadfastly in prayer, being watchful in it with thanksgiving" (Colossians 4:2). He tells them to be "abounding in thankfulness" (Colossians 2:7).

He teaches, "Rejoice always, pray without ceasing, give thanks in all circumstances; for this is the will of God in Christ Jesus for you" (1 Thessalonians 5:16–18).

When we set our minds on prayer and thankfulness, we are fulfilling the will of God for our lives.

But in all circumstances? Always? For everything?

Yes. This is the standard God has set. This is Christian maturity.

As we pursue contentment, we begin to look at every circumstance with so much satisfaction in God Himself that we become thankful for the trials, struggles, pain, and heartache. We grow convinced that God has our best interest in mind and that everything He allows is to make us like Jesus. We should want to be thankful for every experience, not just in hindsight but as we walk through those circumstances.

Remember, we are talking about our minds, not our feelings. We do not only thank God when we feel like it; we thank Him in all things. We master our minds to be obedient to Scripture.

All of this—rejoicing in the Lord always, being anxious for nothing but in everything praying with thankfulness—is Christlikeness. This is the ideal. This is the lifelong destination of our growth. God knows we are imperfect. He knows we fear, doubt, worry, and direct our minds inward. He knows this and still guides us and directs us to improve. He gently urges us through the indwelling Holy Spirit to do a little better each day. Be gracious to yourself as you continue to be a work in progress. Be honest in your failings—because we all have them—and give God glory for His work.

It takes tremendous self-control to master our minds. Not self-will, but the Holy Spirit's work to produce the fruit of self-control. It takes self-control to rejoice in the Lord, to focus on the character of God when our minds start to "what if," to pray without ceasing, to present requests to God in faith that He knows best, to be thankful at all times and in every circumstance. To be content—experience the peace of resting in God—we need the peace of God which surpasses understanding to guard our hearts and minds in Christ Jesus (Philippians 4:7).

I trust that as I do the work of being obedient, He is doing the lion's share of work in my heart and mind. I trust that as I am intentional in mastering my mind to follow this piece of Scripture, He is intentional in making me more like Christ through the process.

Many Christians put a little effort into these practices (rejoicing, remembering, goodness/reasonableness, not being anxious, praying, thankfulness) but give up after a time. I want to offer a loving encouragement to stick with them. First, your goal should not be perfection. We are all miles from perfect. Your goal should be improvement. Little by little, day by day, focus on these practices in small increments. We are moving the mountain of old ways of thinking, lifelong habits, inclinations, and ingrained nature. It will take time and careful thought. Even using a bulldozer, it would take time to move a mountain. Most of us are using shovels or spoons. Be patient with yourself. But keep going. God's grace has covered you. He knows what mountain you are up against. He is in the working. Do your part by being intentional with your thoughts.

SIXTEEN

Think on These (Part 1)

"FINALLY, brothers, whatever is true, whatever is honorable, whatever is just, whatever is pure, whatever is lovely, whatever is commendable, if there is any excellence, if there is anything worthy of praise, think about these things" (Philippians 4:8).

Sometimes I wish I had a mute button for my own brain. I would like a few minutes of quiet from the noise that goes on inside. Even advice like "quiet your mind" doesn't seem to work for me. At that moment, a neglected thought in the very recesses of my subconscious raises its head and speaks up loud and clear.

Rather than try to stop the chatter, I find that directing it with purpose and intention works better; I am telling my brain what to think, following this list Paul gives.

Think on what is true

I have believed my share of lies. I have told lies. I have listened to lies. I have even hoped in lies. Lies are all around us. Even before the age of media and social media, lies were prevalent. Our enemy is the father of lies; as long as he rules this age, lies will abound (John 8:44). This evil, murderous villain "prowls around like a roaring lion, seeking someone to devour" (1 Peter 5:8). His aim is to "steal and kill and destroy" (John 10:10).

But our good King Jesus *is* the truth. He comes to bring abundant life. He comes to set captives free, including those held captive by lies. He exposes the works of darkness by bringing them out into the light (John 10:10; Luke 4:18; Ephesians 5:13).

Paul urges the Ephesians to "walk as children of light (for the fruit of light is found in all that is good and right and true)" (Ephesians 5:8–9). He also tells them to put on the belt of truth as a piece of God's armor (Ephesians 6:14).

Paul also tells the Philippians to think on what is true. We come to know truth by examining Scripture. The enemy's goal is to keep you doubting God. He will use whatever means necessary to keep you from the truth. God, however, has made His truth plain to us. The psalmist declared, "The sum of your word is truth, and every one of your righteous rules endures forever" (Psalm 119:160). Jesus prayed on behalf of His followers, "Sanctify them in the truth; your word is truth" (John 17:17). When we think on the Word, we are thinking on truth.

If God's Word is our standard of truth, everything we think and believe must be held up to the truth and examined. Any belief that doesn't align with Scripture is a lie and must be abandoned. Every sermon, book, song, message, or opinion we take in must be examined. Even mine. Please, compare what I have written with Scripture! If I have written anything contrary to the Word, let me know. I want to be truthful and write in accordance with Scripture!

To think on truth, you must be reading God's Word or hearing God's Word daily. Multiple times a day even. If you are too busy to read God's Word, you are too busy. You are believing a lie that whatever you are doing is more important than God's Word.

Truth is found in God's Word. Truth is found in the Word made flesh, "who dwelt among us, . . . full of grace and truth" (John 1:14). Think on whatever is true.

Think on what is honorable

This Greek word transliterated *semnos* means "august, venerable, reverend, to be venerated for character, honorable."[1]

This is a tricky word to define in modern terms. But I love words and definitions. I went on a long rabbit hole through the dictionary to come up with a definition: anything that reflects the majestic dignity and grandeur of God; the dignity of His image bearers; the transformation of His followers through sanctification; or the fruit of a life lived seeking wisdom, application of the Word, and integrity.[2]

The honorable is all around us.

God's Word is filled with honorable men and women. As you read Scripture, look to the majesty of God. Think on the good work God is doing in purifying us, making us worthy of the call to salvation we have received! The greatest works of literature are filled with honorable characters. Think on the characters in the books you read. What makes the heroes honorable? Reflect on the dignity of the authors of nonfiction you read. Read biographies of saints who went before us, or talk to the older believers in your church. Your church is filled with honorable men and women. They are worth honor because of their devotion to the Lord.

In our flesh, we are more drawn to the dishonorable. We prefer to look for where our brothers and sisters are failing, to see lives that are falling apart so we can feel better about our own failings. As God works in us, He redeems us from such dishonorable thinking. We can see people through His eyes, not our own. We can respond with grief and compassion for their struggles, rather than an insatiable appetite for sordid details.

Each person is made in the image of God. We are commanded here to think of them with the honor due an image bearer, looking for where God is at work in their lives. We are to glorify God by honoring His creation as worthy of respect.

Think on what is just

God alone is just. He is the One who defines right and wrong. He is the only One who is right and righteous in all His ways. He sets the standard.

We are more prone to think of justice in terms of fairness or equity. And most often, our judgments are tainted by what would most benefit us.

We stand before God as completely unjust beings. We are not righteous. Not one of us. Therefore, we have no bearing toward rightness. When we are justified by the only just One, we are made right in His eyes.

We still see through human eyes, with a narrow worldview and limited experiences. Thinking about justice from God's perspective is a lifelong pursuit. To think on whatever is just is to think on what God says is just, to think on His standard of right and wrong.

When Jesus walked this earth, He fulfilled God's requirements perfectly. He is our example of the One who lived out Micah 6:8: "He has told you, O man, what is good; and what does the Lord require of you but to do justice, and to love kindness, and to walk humbly with your God?"

Jesus is the only one to live on this earth with perfect justice. He saw mankind through the eternal eyes of Godhood. He could see people for who they were, even the secret thoughts of the heart. He loved extravagantly, forgave sins, called out the hypocrisy of the religious elite.

John 8 records an interaction that demonstrates Christ's justice. A woman was caught in the act of adultery. The scribes and Pharisees had brought her before Jesus as He sat teaching a crowd. The religious leaders demanded justice according to the Law of Moses. Well, they demanded only part of the justice the Law called for. Leviticus 20:10 states that *both* the man and the woman are to be stoned for committing adultery. Surely, if the woman was caught in the act, she was not alone, right? It is plain to see the scribes and Pharisees were claiming to want justice but were hoping to trap Jesus by creating a public spectacle.

Jesus did not fall for their trap. He said, "Let him who is without sin among you be the first to throw a stone at her" (John 8:7). Jesus, the only individual in this entire scene who was without sin, knew the hearts and sins of every person before Him. He could, by all rights, pick up stones against all of them. But He didn't. He let their own consciences speak to them. One by one, they walked away.

When the crowd of accusers was gone, Jesus faced this ashamed woman. He called her sin what it was; He told her to go and sin no more. He did not condemn her. He was without sin and, by His own statement, had the right to stone her. But Jesus did not come into the world "to condemn the world, but in order that the world might be saved through him" (John 3:17).

Through Jesus, our sin record is removed. We are justified. When I justify my bank account, I am making sure my ledger and the bank's ledger equal out to zero difference. God justifies us through Jesus by removing our negative balance of sin, zeroing it out because of Jesus' blood. He took all our sin upon Himself, and His righteousness is added to our account, as a positive balance. God is just because payment was due for our sin. He is the justifier because He applies Jesus' payment on our behalf.

We can spend our whole lives reflecting on the justification of our sins and never run out of things to learn. It is a wonderful, marvelous mystery worth thinking on!

Think on what is pure

I love a winter landscape. I appreciate how the newly fallen snow looks covering everything in pure, sparkling white. I especially liked to see the effects of "ice fog" when we lived in South Dakota. The fog would lift, revealing completely white pine trees. Not just snow on the branches, but every needle coated in a white layer of crystalline ice. It was dramatic and beautiful.

The purity of Jesus stands in stark contrast to the world of our familiar landscape; He stands alone as *pure*. In telling us to think on whatsoever is pure, Paul is bringing us back to the holy, blameless, spotless life of Jesus. God's purity and holiness are unreachable for our finite brains. It is difficult enough to grasp God made flesh, walking among us, with all the temptations common to man, yet without sin. That is something to think on indeed!

But also, think on the purifying effect Jesus has on the life of His followers. It isn't the snow that fascinates me; it is the effect of the snow on the familiar. The landscapes of human lives are forever changed by the life-giving purity of Jesus.

God will make me like Christ—completely pure—when Christ returns. John puts it this way: "Beloved, we are God's children now, and what we will be has not yet appeared; but we know that when he appears we shall be like him, because we shall see him as he is. And everyone who thus hopes in him purifies himself as he is pure" (1 John 3:2–3).

Think on the indwelling of the Holy Spirit, who was sent to guide you into righteous living. The pure *Holy* Spirit of God, dwelling in you and me. Rather than being tainted by our flesh, His power enables *us* to be more like Him.

Think on the purity of a newborn baby. Though babies are born with a sin nature, as we hold them, we sense the purity of one who has not yet done anything sinful. We breathe in the fresh scent of their newness (there is nothing on this earth that compares to the scent of a new baby!). We have been made new through our belief in Jesus Christ; we have new life, new roles in the world, new purpose (2 Corinthians 5:17–21). We have a new smell too! We are the aroma of Christ. We smell like new life—new, pure life—to each other (2 Corinthians 2:14–16).

SEVENTEEN

Think on These (Part 2)

LET'S continue examining the commands Paul gives in Philippians 4:8.

Think on what is lovely

Lovely is such a lovely word. It just has a beauty and grace of its own.

Philippians 4:8 is the only time this word is used in the Bible. This is presumed to be a compound of the word *phileo*—"brotherly love"—and the preposition *pros*—"toward, in the direction of, between," etc.[1]

Most literally, then, it would mean "friendly toward." Think on whatever you see that makes you friendly toward God and others; think on that which stirs your affections. Think on what is pleasant. Think on the undefinable qualities of beauty you find in the world around you.

Think on the lovely qualities in others. What about another person stirs your brotherly affection toward them? With most people I feel a deep affection for, it would be hard to pinpoint what it is about them. They are a sum of their traits. There is time, shared experiences, and devotion to each other. There is a certain "je ne sais quoi" about those I love, qualities I can't name or describe. There is just *something* about them. They are just lovely.

There is so much that is lovely around us in art, literature, nature, in the world at large. There are landscapes that inspire a hushed peace. I have read books with such beautifully written characters that stir an affection or a desire to be like that character. Paintings draw me in with their emotion captured in colors on canvas. All around us is a world drawing us to deeper affection for God and others.

Think on what is commendable

Here we come to another word that is only used this one time. Commendable. This means "of good report, spoken of favorably, or things spoken in a kindly spirit, with good will towards others."[2]

This word is challenging because, like honorable, it is completely against our nature. We are highly prone to think poorly of others. The news is full of the details of moral failings, misadventures, crimes, and scandals. Character attacks and doom and gloom plague us.

These are not the things we should be thinking on. There is nothing commendable about exploits of the fallen world around us. We should be thinking about the best in others. We should be thinking favorably of them. If we cannot think favorably, we should be praying for them, not participating in the revelry at their expense.

It takes considerable effort and a work of the Holy Spirit to apply this Scripture.

I consciously look for things to think well of in the people around me, while overlooking the scandalous. I try to ask myself, "Would I want someone thinking—or worse, talking—about this area of my life if it were me?" Obviously I would not, so why should I do unto another that which I do not want done to me? I want people to think well of me. I want to think well of others too.

The part of the definition that gives me the most pause is the "kindly spirit" and "good will towards others." In thinking of what is commendable, we are looking at others with kind eyes, having compassion toward them, and wanting the best for them. It is seeking the best *in* them, with a spirit of pursuing the best *for* them. God working in someone's life is the most commendable thing we can think of. Any time we see the commendable character of Jesus in someone, we should think on that with praise!

Think on any excellence

Many Bible translations use the words virtue and excellence interchangeably. The English Standard Version uses the word *virtue* here. The virtues encompass moral excellence. To have moral excellence, one must display the virtues.

Virtue is an archaic word in our culture, isn't it?

If it is an archaic word, it is certainly an archaic concept. Yet here we are, commanded in Scripture to think on these things. More than that, Peter says, "For this very reason, make every effort to supplement your faith with virtue" (2 Peter 1:5). Pay close attention to what he says next. "For if these qualities are yours and are increasing, they keep you from being ineffective or unfruitful in the knowledge of our Lord Jesus Christ. For whoever lacks these qualities is so nearsighted that he is blind, having forgotten that he was cleansed from his former sins" (2 Peter 1:8–9).

God calls us to His glory and excellence (2 Peter 1:3). He expects us to add to our faith excellence. God is the definition of moral character. All virtues are found in Him. Therefore, to show His glory, we must add virtue to our lives.

I want to be effective and fruitful in my knowledge of Jesus Christ. I do not want to be blind and forgetful. Therefore, I must possess these qualities in increasing measure.

So . . . what are the virtues?

A virtue is an inner attitude or disposition that demonstrates itself in outward behavior. It is consistent, habitual, lifelong practice. These traits can include diligence, cheerfulness, contentment, prudence, wisdom, humility, courage, kindness, loyalty, chastity, modesty, gratitude, and patience.[3] This is far from an exhaustive list of virtues, but for the sake of the practice of thinking on excellence, this is a good start.

A virtuous person seeks to live their life in a manner consistent with these traits and is repentant when they fall short. These virtues are demonstrated in the life of our Lord Jesus; they are to be ours. We are to look for them in others as well.

Think on anything worthy of praise

This word *praise* means formal or official approval, commendation, or praise, and it is slightly different from the word for praise offered in worship. It is used to describe the praise God will give to the one whose heart is circumcised, who is a Jew inwardly by faith and by the Spirit, and to describe the commendation a ruler would bestow upon the good conduct of a citizen (Romans 2:29; 13:3). Peter uses it in 1 Peter 1:7 to remind us that the testing of our faith, if it is genuine, will "result in praise and glory and honor at the revelation of Jesus Christ."

There are things we do—and things others do—that are worthy of praise. God Himself will praise us for things we do in His name. Everything we do that brings us praise and commendation will ultimately bring God praise and glory.

Think on conduct that would merit commendation. Think on this conduct in others. Think on what Christ did that is worthy of all approval and praise.

If we see something that is praiseworthy—deserving of commendation—and we are not inclined to praise, it is time for a heart check. It is always an indication there is something out of alignment within us, not something wrong with the object receiving praise. A lack of praise response to something praiseworthy is revealing an insecurity or jealousy, perhaps an anxious spirit, something we need to address in self-examination and repentance.

EIGHTEEN

Whatever and Any

YOU MAY BE LOOKING at these "think on these" items and wondering how to apply them in the nitty-gritty of your day-to-day life. Of course, the Sunday school answer is Jesus. Think on Jesus.

But how?

Paul uses the "whatever" and "any" intentionally. We live in a world filled with the general revelation of God. If anything draws to mind one of these qualities, think on it.

I attended an unorthodox elementary school. We had a lot of natural learning experiences. We spent a lot of time camping, hiking, spelunking, and going to museums and galleries. We had guest instructors and special projects. The premise was a student-led educational theory: if you provide a child with opportunities and engaging resources, they will learn naturally. You can take advantage of a child's natural curiosity to engage their mind.

As a student educated in this environment, as well as traditional curriculum-led systems, I can attest that it is much easier to learn and grow if you direct your attention along lines of interest and curiosity that already exist.

You probably have interests and hobbies. You have natural inclinations. We live in a world of endless possibilities. Tap into your natural interests (of course, I am only encouraging honorable interests) to explore the world around you, searching for these things Paul encourages.

Perhaps you are interested in sports, history, nature, biographies, cooking, industry, automotive, art, poetry, architecture, music, science . . . whatever! You can find true, honorable, just, pure, lovely, commendable, virtuous, and praiseworthy things to think on within your interests. Look for them. You will start seeing them.

Why?

What we think on matters because contentment is an intellectual state. In fact, much of our spiritual maturity and growth take place because of the way we think.

We are more likely to use what we can access easily, both in life and in terms of our ways of thinking. We are more likely to *be* true, honorable, just, pure, lovely, commendable, virtuous, and praiseworthy when we are thinking on these attributes since it keeps them on our minds. I have found, as I have been attempting to apply this to my own life, that the more I think on the things Paul lists, the more accessible they are.

The writer of Hebrews talks about the maturity that comes from training our minds. He begins by stating that the audience of his letter is immature, needing milk when they should be ready for solid food. He then says, "But solid food is for the mature, for those who have their powers of discernment trained by constant practice to distinguish good from evil" (Hebrews 5:14). By constantly practicing intentional thought, we can more easily access the power of discernment. We keep the "good" that we think on at the forefront of our minds so that the evil is more recognizable.

As you focus on the truth, lies will become more evident. As you think on whatever is honorable—the dignity and respectability—in others, any activity that leads you to think of your fellow man in dishonor becomes repulsive. As you move through the rest of the list —just, pure, lovely, commendable, excellent, and praiseworthy— you will begin to get a sense of these qualities acting as guardrails of sorts. If something brings impure thoughts or foolish desires (as opposed to the chastity and temperance virtues), then you can consciously make the choice not to participate in those activities. By becoming aware of what you are thinking on, you can also become more aware of the thoughts you should not allow to linger.

Paul was not a "do as I say, not as I do" kind of teacher. He worked to live a life that was worth following. He knew that as an apostle of the Lord Jesus Christ, he was the example of what it meant to live a life worthy of the gospel. He was the example for other believers to follow.

"What you have learned and received and heard and seen in me —practice these things" (Philippians 4:9). Paul was all-in: faithful, devoted, and diligent. He took a hard line on correct doctrine and correct living, balancing it with love and grace. Paul's sole aim was to see the kingdom of God advance. Read Paul's story in the book of Acts. Read his letters. Follow his example. He was a man, just like us. He still faced struggles against the flesh, temptations, fears, and failures. He understood the value of an example in human form.

The fact is, there are principles in the Bible that can be difficult to grasp until you see someone living them out. It can be difficult to understand what it means to live the Christian life without an example to follow. What does it look like to follow Christ as a student, in dating, as a stay-at-home mom, as an employee, as a boss, as a neighbor, in a retirement home, as a church member? We all need examples. And we all need to remember that we *are* examples. We need to be intentional about seeking someone to follow, someone who lives the Christian life, walking in a manner worthy of the gospel. We also need to be intentional about being an example to someone else (Titus 2:1–10).

So, what does all this have to do with contentment? Why spend this much time focusing on what we think and reflect on? Philippians 4:9 ends with this: "and the God of peace will be with you." It is remarkable to note that, when we think on the right things, our hearts and minds will be guarded with the peace of God that passes understanding by the God of peace! This peace is our "why" for giving attention to our thoughts, our contemplation.

Many of us want the peace of God that passes understanding more than we want the God of peace. We want the benefit He offers without wanting Him. This may be the reason peace is so elusive. As we are intentional with our thinking, God is at work in our hearts and minds. Paul reminds us that the Lord is at hand. He is always with us.

Rejoice in the Lord. Always. Rejoice a little more. Be reasonable, good, gentle. Remember that the Lord is at hand. Think on His return and His nearness. Remember His faithfulness to keep His promises. Do not be anxious. Pray about everything. Be exceedingly thankful. Think on what is true, honorable, just, pure, lovely, commendable, virtuous, worthy of praise. Follow Paul's example.

Be guarded by God's peace. Know that the God of peace is with you. Isaiah 26:3 gives us this reminder of God's peace for His people, a song of praise to God: "You keep him in perfect peace whose mind is stayed on you, because he trusts in you." Being kept "in perfect peace" sounds like contentment to me.

Contentment is dependent on learning to think as God thinks. God's ways are so high above and beyond our human capacity to understand. We use the word *transcendent* to try to grasp God's holy separation from humanity. Transcendent means going beyond ordinary limits, surpassing, exceeding. Because God is the Creator, He is separate from His creation. He is outside time, space, nature, and, honestly, comprehension. His ways are otherworldly, incomparable, supernatural, preeminent, and supreme.

He tells us, "My thoughts are not your thoughts, neither are your ways my ways, declares the LORD. For as the heavens are higher than the earth, so are my ways higher than your ways and my thoughts than your thoughts" (Isaiah 55:8–9). Many times in Scripture, the rhetorical question is asked, "Who can understand the mind of the Lord?"

To be transformed by the renewing of our minds; to set our minds on the things above, on things of the Spirit, not things of the flesh; to be renewed in the spirit of our minds and put on the new self; to have the mind of Christ be in us; to have the peace of God and the God of peace to guard our hearts and minds, we must learn to think as God thinks. Well, as much as a human brain can. We must learn to honor His way of thinking above our own.

Before Christ, my mind was fashioned by the world. Every thought, wish, hope, or decision was based on a mixture of messages from a world hell-bent on defying God, my own delusions, and a self-will decidedly intent on self-rule. Not one of those elements produces peace with God nor any semblance of satisfaction in God. Because of Christ, I am a new creation. I am given a heart of flesh where stone once prevailed. I am given a new mind—Christ's own—and have had the law written upon my heart and mind to be guided and directed by the Holy Spirit. Contentment has only been made possible because of this transformation.

We can only be content when we are fully convinced of the rightness of God's way of thinking. We may not always be able to understand it (in fact, His Word says we will not), but we can be sure of it. We can trust His ways are not only higher than ours but better. We will find contentment when we are sure that in His wisdom and knowledge God has done all things right, trusting in the perfection and holiness of His very nature.

Part Four

CONTENTMENT IN CONFLICT

NINETEEN

Paul's Conflicts

IN WRITING, it is important to have a good introduction to your chapters, a "hook," so to speak, to engage your readers and get them interested in what you are about to say.

I cannot find a good way to introduce the topic of conflict. Conflict stinks. There is no heartwarming illustration, no poem, nothing I can use to "hook" you to make you want to read about conflict.

I do not even *want* to write about it. I am probably the least qualified person to write about contentment in conflict because I absolutely detest conflict. It unsettles me. I might even be a little phobic about conflict.

Paul brings up five different conflicts within this little book of Philippians. Five conflicts in four chapters. And yet Paul was content.

I guess this means I need to write this section, and hopefully you are interested enough to see what the world's most conflict-adverse writer has to say about finding contentment in conflict.

Since contentment is peace and stillness of spirit, it seems unlikely that contentment and conflict can coexist. The world tells us peace is the absence of conflict. Since their inception, beauty pageant contestants and politicians have made world peace their promised effect of being selected. We celebrate peace treaties which end armed conflict. We want peaceful neighborhoods. Peaceful schools. Just peace.

I want to be at peace. Peace is my core, motivating value. Therefore, conflict causes my blood pressure to spike. It causes that feeling in the pit of my stomach, kind of like butterflies but not in a good way. Studying how Paul addresses these conflicts gives us a better path to peace than the pageant queens and politicians offer.

Opposition to the Gospel

I have a feeling Paul was not as conflict phobic as I am. He was pretty bold. Okay, that's an understatement. Paul was *really* bold!

But I wonder how he truly felt. I read his story in the book of Acts with more than a hint of astonishment. This man was violently opposed almost everywhere he went because he preached the gospel. *Violently* opposed. *Everywhere* he went.

When Paul met the Philippians, he had been beaten and imprisoned, which led to the Philippian jailer and his whole household coming to faith in Christ (Acts 16:25–34). Paul was "asked" to leave Philippi. As he traveled from city to city, he received similar treatment. His opposition started following him as he traveled, stirring up angry mobs to protest his preaching.

In the final encounter that led to his imprisonment, he was falsely accused, almost ripped to pieces by a mob, rescued by the Romans, who promptly beat him for needing to be rescued. He finally got sent to Rome under guard, where the book of Acts concludes.

When Paul writes to the Philippians, "I want you to know, brothers, that what has happened to me has really served to advance the gospel," he is talking about very serious opposition to his work *for the gospel* (Philippians 1:12). Paul had been opposed at every turn.

Because the gospel is opposed by the world.

But Paul takes heart in this opposition. He continues, "so that it has become known throughout the whole imperial guard and to all the rest that my imprisonment is for Christ. And most of the brothers, having become confident in the Lord by my imprisonment, are much more bold to speak the word without fear" (Philippians 1:13–14).

What does Luke record about Paul's imprisonment? "He lived there two whole years at his own expense, and welcomed all who came to him, proclaiming the kingdom of God and teaching about the Lord Jesus Christ with all boldness and without hindrance" (Acts 28:30–31). No wonder he spoke boldly and without hindrance! His opponents had tried to kill him, practically ripping him apart, yet it had served to get him to Rome, the very place he wished to go! What else were they going to do? Succeed in killing him? He wanted to go to Christ's presence more than Rome, so that would have been an even greater win for this apostle.

Not only did his opponents accomplish for him his heart's desire, but he also had a captive audience during his, well, captivity. He had regular guards assigned to him. There is some speculation he could have had a guard chained to him or even just assigned to guard the house Paul lived in. We do not have the details, but the whole imperial guard knew Paul was imprisoned because of his faith in Christ. He ends his letter to the Philippians with a greeting from all the saints, "especially those of Caesar's household" (Philippians 4:22).

Stop and think about the absolute absurdity of the marvelous work of God! This is jaw-dropping information, and Paul slips it in casually as if it were no big deal. Saints. In Caesar's household. The whole imperial guard and Caesar's household had been impacted eternally because of Paul's imprisonment.

The nearby believers had been emboldened by his imprisonment. They were sharing the gospel more freely and with more confidence. Imagine having access to Paul during his imprisonment. Imagine telling him you're afraid to share the gospel. I imagine he would laugh a little. "Why? Are you afraid of becoming like me?" I imagine his face beaming with joy as he holds up his chains.

Paul served as an example of facing the opponents of Christ

boldly. There are examples from every generation; the gospel has been opposed throughout its entire existence.

Though Paul talks very nonchalantly about his opponents, he speaks strongly to his readers about how to face theirs. He says,

> Only let your manner of life be worthy of the gospel of Christ, so that whether I come and see you or am absent, I may hear of you that you are standing firm in one spirit, with one mind striving side by side for the faith of the gospel, and not frightened in anything by your opponents. This is a clear sign to them of their destruction, but of your salvation, and that from God. For it has been granted to you that for the sake of Christ you should not only believe in him but also suffer for his sake, engaged in the same conflict that you saw I had and now hear that I still have. (Philippians 1:27–30)

Reread the last sentence. I do not want conflict and suffering granted to me. But it is truth. We need to accept that to believe in Jesus Christ is to go against the ways of the world; it is to invite opposition. The truth is—the *promise* is—we will face persecution (Matthew 5:10–12; John 15:18–16:4; 16:33; 2 Timothy 3:12; 1 Peter 4:12–19; 1 John 3:13).

But what happens when you are not frightened by your opponents? What happens when you stand firmly in your faith in Jesus? Paul says this becomes a clear sign to them that your salvation is from God. And it becomes clear to them that they are facing destruction.

Paul reminds the Ephesians that we are not fighting against flesh and blood, but against spiritual powers, and urges them to put on the full armor of God. But he also reminds them, "You were dead in the trespasses and sins in which you once walked, following the course of this world, following the prince of the power of the air, the spirit that is now at work in the sons of disobedience" (Ephesians 2:1–2). This is an important reminder because apart from Christ we are all opponents of the gospel. We were all capable of being persecutors. We were all capable of fiercely fighting against the ones who walk in the truth.

Paul tells the Thessalonians that he boasts about their persecutions and all the suffering they are enduring: "This is evidence of the righteous judgment of God, that you may be considered worthy of the kingdom of God, for which you are also suffering" (2 Thessalonians 1:5). He reminds them that there will come a time of fiery judgment for those who oppose the gospel. This is in part to comfort them that God sees their affliction and will punish those who inflict it. It also serves as a reminder to have compassion on your persecutors.

You read that right. Have compassion on your persecutors. They are opposing you—the gospel in you—because they are blinded. They are deceived. They are following the prince of this world to their destruction.

It should be with great humility we face our opponents. We were once just like them. We should still be just like them. But God has done tremendous work in our lives. He has saved us, washed us, regenerated us, renewed us, poured out His Holy Spirit on us, justified us, made us heirs, and given us the hope of eternal life.

Our opponents have none of that. They are still separated from Christ, having no hope and living without God in this world (Ephesians 2:12). No wonder they oppose our message. It is foreign to them. It is, frankly, crazy to them.

Paul himself communicates a feeling of being close to Christ because of suffering for the gospel (Philippians 3:10). He assures the Thessalonians that they are experiencing the same suffering at the hands of their countrymen that Paul and the prophets—and our Lord Jesus—all suffered (1 Thessalonians 2:14–16).

We are in good company indeed. For Jesus said, "If the world hates you, know that it has hated me before it hated you. If you were of the world, the world would love you as its own; but because you are not of the world, but I chose you out of the world, therefore the world hates you" (John 15:18–19). You are not greater than your master. The world hates your master. Why shouldn't it hate you?

The reason for peace with God—deep, inner, stillness of

contentment—while facing the conflict of those who oppose the gospel is found in 1 Peter 4:19: "Therefore let those who suffer according to God's will entrust their souls to a faithful Creator while doing good." God has a firm grasp on your soul. What does it matter if men hate you? What does it matter if they revile you? Taunt you?

But what does it matter if your steadfastness and gentleness open their eyes to the truth of the gospel? What does it matter if the one who violently opposes you because of the gospel becomes a believer? Isn't that possibility worth enduring shame, torture, imprisonment, or even death? What a great and merciful God we serve! All of us were His enemies, and He has made us His children. Even the vilest offender, like Paul, is called to receive mercy and grace and be loved lavishly by God. He urges us to correct our opponents with gentleness because God may "grant them repentance leading to a knowledge of the truth . . . and escape from the snare of the devil" (2 Timothy 2:25–26).

Have you ever stopped to consider that Paul died for the faith he once tried to snuff out? Imagine the rejoicing in heaven when he came to faith in Christ! Imagine the heartfelt welcome when he joined the other martyrs in heaven, including the martyrs he was responsible for sending before him. We can trust our souls to God— and the souls of our opponents—knowing that He is good, loving, and gracious, and He gives far more mercy than we deserve.

God has prepared a special place in heaven for those who are martyred for the sake of the gospel. Revelation 6:9–11 reveals they wait and rest under the altar. There were two altars in the tabernacle, the earthly representation of the heavenly throne room. It is unspecified if the altar the martyrs are under is the altar of sacrifice or the altar of incense; however, in Revelation 8:1–5, the altar of incense is referred to as "the altar" and the prayer of the saints is mixed with the incense that goes up before the throne. In the tabernacle, this altar would have been directly in front of the curtain that separated the holy place from the most holy place; the most holy place was where the mercy seat—God's throne—was kept. It is remarkable that God keeps the souls of those martyred directly in front of His throne in heaven. Indeed, "Precious in the sight of the LORD is the death of his saints."

Regardless of what our opponents bring against us, we can be content in the conflict because we bring glory to the God who guards our souls.

TWENTY

Those Who Pervert the Gospel

IT IS difficult to put ourselves in first-century sandals in order to fully understand many of the difficulties the early Christians faced. The church was born within the Roman Empire, which was as diverse as it was powerful. Rome had a pride in their era of peace, called the *Pax Romana*, which came at the tip of the spear. Roman diversity was lauded, though the expectation of allegiance to Caesar was homogenous.

The church was born in Judea, the land of the Israelites, among Jews who saw the Messiah Jesus as fulfilling centuries of prophecy. Then the church spread to the surrounding areas. These were Gentiles finding faith in a God they may not have experienced before, particularly those coming from polytheistic cultures.

They lived in this tension of something entirely *new*. Never in the history of the world had God become man, lived a sinless life, been killed, and resurrected. Never had the God of the Israelites commanded the separate, set-apart people to *go* into all the world and make followers in all the nations. And while Jesus was a Jew, born under the Law of Moses, He was not sending out His followers to make converts to Judaism; He sent them out to make disciples of Himself.

All of us who are born again into this faith in Jesus are born into a faith that is shaped and informed by the faith of the Jews. We are part of a faith that was the fulfillment of promises and prophecies. Everything we believe was given context in the faith of those who went before us.

But, as a fulfilled prophecy, it is set aside. We are no longer looking for the Messiah: He has come. We are no longer offering sacrifices; He was the final sacrifice upon the eternal altar of God. We no longer have atonement and purification rituals; we have been atoned for and made pure. No longer is there a dividing wall between the access the Jews have to God and the access of the Gentiles—in fact, not even a dividing curtain between the access of the High Priest and the access of the common Jew. All are torn down. We are given equal access through the blood of Jesus.

What do we do with the Law and the prophets? What do we do with centuries of history and heritage?

These were the questions the early church faced. When it was just a group of Jews-turned-Christians, the answer was quite simple: go on as normal, worshiping Jesus as the risen Savior who fulfilled the Law. As we read the first few chapters of Acts, regarding the earliest years after Jesus ascended into heaven, we see the first generation of believers doing just that. We see their lives centered around Jerusalem, with a continued presence in the Temple. We see them gathering together, living as Jews, honoring what we now call Sunday as the Lord's Day, building a community together of like-minded fellowship.

Eventually, the church began to realize that God was doing something different. The Holy Spirit fell upon Gentiles who responded to Peter's preaching in the same dramatic fashion it had fallen upon the first believers in Jerusalem at Pentecost. Peter reported what happened to the rest of the church leadership in Jerusalem: "And they glorified God, saying, 'Then to the Gentiles also God has granted repentance that leads to life'" (Acts 11:18).

It was bad enough to the Jewish leaders that this rabble-rousing crowd of nobodies was following a man they had executed, but it was unthinkable that they were now recruiting Gentiles, telling them they had equal—and better—standing with God as these lifelong law-keeping zealots!

The Jews were convinced that the outward expression of holiness —represented in circumcision—was all that mattered. Through the power of the Holy Spirit, believers in Jesus are given a circumcised heart, a heart of flesh with the Law written upon it. We are given holiness and righteousness because of the holiness and righteousness of Jesus; therefore, it is not dependent upon our ability to keep the Law.

Holiness and righteous living are important. However, they are powered and motivated by the Holy Spirit living within us, flowing out of our justification *already received*. We are *made holy* through the ongoing, lifelong process of sanctification because of the working of God in our lives. To the Jew, you *work at* being holy and righteous so that your sins may be few and your atonement secured. As Paul says in Romans 9:32, the Jews were pursuing a righteousness from works, not from faith. The difference is motivation, not action.

Paul warns the Philippians to be on their guard against these Jews. "Look out for the dogs, look out for the evildoers, look out for those who mutilate the flesh" (Philippians 3:2). You might think it is a little harsh for Paul to call these people dogs and evildoers, but the purity of the gospel is on the line. Either the gospel is enough to save us, or it isn't. There is no halfway option.

Paul understood this concept better than anyone else. He *had* believed wholeheartedly in the Jewish plan of salvation, working zealously for his own righteousness. Remember, Paul tried to eradicate the Jews who strayed from this belief. He persecuted the early Christians—who still identified as Jews—because he saw them as polluting the truth of Judaism. When his eyes were opened (literally), he saw that there was no way to earn your salvation.

Paul continues in Philippians, "For we are the circumcision, who worship by the Spirit of God and glory in Christ Jesus and put no confidence in the flesh—though I myself have reason for confidence in the flesh also. If anyone else thinks he has reason for confidence in the flesh, I have more: circumcised on the eighth day, of the people of Israel, of the tribe of Benjamin, a Hebrew of Hebrews; as to the law, a Pharisee; as to zeal, a persecutor of the church; as to right-eousness under the law, blameless" (Philippians 3:3–6). Paul is saying, "If anyone could have been saved under the Jewish system, it was me! But even I couldn't." Why would you want to go to a system that *could not* save you, especially after receiving the grace and mercy of Jesus Christ that *are* adequate to save?

This matter was so important to Paul that the entire letter to the Galatians is devoted to it. He addresses it directly and indirectly throughout the book of Romans. He addresses unity among the Jewish and Gentile believers in the letter to the Ephesians, since both were dead in their trespasses before Christ and both were saved by grace through faith, *not of works*. He mentions this matter in the books of Colossians and 1 Timothy. The writer of Hebrews is urging the Christians of Jewish heritage to move away from the practices and rituals they have depended upon and move toward the Christian community—go outside the camp—distancing themselves from the Jews. James and Jude also speak to this in their letters.

If the matter of purity of the gospel is of the utmost importance when it comes to the practices the earliest believers originated from, how much more important it is to guard the purity of the gospel against the perversion that comes from blending the gospel with other faiths. As people were getting saved out of various forms of idol worship or Hellenistic philosophy, it was easy to think of Christ as an addition to the various faiths already being practiced. There is no room for "Jesus and" anywhere in the doctrine of salvation. Paul addresses this in the books of Romans, 1 and 2 Corinthians, Ephesians, Colossians, 1 Thessalonians, and 1 and 2 Timothy. 2 Peter and Jude both address the issues of false teachers and the purity of the gospel. Paul said, "But whatever gain I had, I counted as loss for the sake of Christ. Indeed, I count everything as loss because of the surpassing worth of knowing Christ Jesus my Lord. For his sake, I have suffered the loss of all things and count them as rubbish, in order that I may gain Christ and be found in him, not having a righteousness of my own that comes from the law, but that which comes from faith in Christ, the righteousness from God that depends on faith" (Philippians 3:7–9). The comparison of life before

Christ and life in Christ was not even worth making. Though Paul came from a Jewish background, the same could be said for any accomplishments done in the flesh or in pursuit of a false god. They are worth nothing. In fact, they are rubbish. That's a nice way of saying excrement. Poo. The only thing they are good for is being thrown to the dogs who eat trash in the street.

Why on Earth would we want to add our rubbish (whatever we count our accomplishments) to the salvation ledger? It is like saying, "Gee, Jesus, thanks for salvation, but I think it is lacking a little excrement to make it complete!" How ridiculous!

Salvation is through Jesus alone, by grace alone, through faith alone. There is one God, one Mediator, one way to the Father. There are no works or human efforts you can add to the equation.

Paul is so adamant on this topic that he tells the Galatians, if anyone, even an angel or Paul himself, were to preach a different gospel, he would be cursed (Galatians 1:8–9).

You might be thinking, "I do not have anyone preaching a different gospel to me, so this doesn't really apply to me." You would be thinking wrong.

The purity of the gospel is so important that our enemy will continue to pervert it in whatever way he can dream up. Our culture is overrun with perversions of the gospel. Any version of Christianity blending faith with Christ and any other faith, watering down the exclusivity of faith alone in Christ alone, blending works, effort, achievement, nationalism, indulgence, or any other corruption, is not the gospel.

Our culture will twist and pervert our faith to make those who follow the genuine gospel appear closed-minded, arrogant, rigid, and hypocritical. Paul's culture twisted his similarly.

So, how do we have contentment when facing this type of conflict?

We have contentment when we know the gospel and believe it. We have contentment when we are confident in the truth of the gospel. We can be content when we remind ourselves daily of the gospel we believe and on which we take our stand.

As Christians, we believe that as Adam's children we are all sinners. As sinners, we deserve spiritual death and eternal separation from God. As sinners, we are incapable of doing anything but sin. It is our very nature. As sinners, we are dead in our trespasses.

We believe that God, because of the great love with which He loved us, God being rich in mercy, God being kind to us beyond all measure, made us alive with Christ. We believe that through faith in Jesus Christ, God gives us eternal life, forgives our sins, pours out His Holy Spirit on us as a Helper, Guide, Teacher, Comforter, with the guarantee of our future inheritance. We believe that after we die, we will be in God's presence. We believe that we are recipients of God's grace, His unmerited favor, which we cannot earn, for otherwise, it would not be grace.

This is the source of our contentment. We have peace with God because God has made us right with Him.

When we face the conflict of those who wish to pervert the gospel, we can maintain our contentment because we maintain our grasp on the truth. Ultimately, anyone who perverts the gospel is an opponent of the gospel. Any belief that deviates from the gospel of the Bible is not truth. We follow the guidelines listed before. We correct our opponents with love and gentleness. We graciously disciple those in our circles of influence. We stand firm. We speak the truth in love. We trust God to open their eyes.

TWENTY-ONE

Those Who Preach the Gospel for Selfish Gain

SOMETIMES I COME to a passage of Scripture and wish I had more details. Sometimes I would like to know more about the people or the circumstances, but the passage we will look at next leaves me wondering, *Why?*

Paul tells the Philippians, "Some indeed preach Christ from envy and rivalry, but others from good will. The latter do it out of love, knowing that I am put here for the defense of the gospel. The former proclaim Christ out of selfish ambition, not sincerely but thinking to afflict me in my imprisonment. What then? Only that in every way, whether in pretense or in truth, Christ is proclaimed, and in that I rejoice" (Philippians 1:15–18). We do not have a lot of information here, do we? This is immediately following Paul's declaration that his imprisonment has given brothers boldness to preach without fear.

The genuine gospel is being preached. Not a distorted version. The true gospel.

But some are using it for their own gain. They are motivated by envy, rivalry, selfish ambition, and a desire to afflict Paul. This is what leaves me scratching my head: how do they think preaching the gospel will afflict Paul?

Unfortunately, as humans with a sin nature, sometimes that sin nature still motivates us. Until the resurrection of our own glorified bodies in heaven, our motives will easily slip to our own, falling from the pure motivation to glorify God and see other sinners receive mercy. Even the most godly, selfless, walking-a-worthy-walk minister of the gospel will be stricken by ill motives. I can guarantee it. (What they do with those motives is another story.)

But God is so good! He takes our best efforts and our less than honorable efforts and our downright most selfishly motivated efforts and works His glorious truth through them. I rejoice that His work is not limited by pure motives! Paul did too. If the pure gospel is being preached, even if it is being preached by those with impure motives, then God's work is being accomplished. That is worthy of rejoicing!

Paul's matter-of-fact handling of this conflict should be our guide. The motives of others are not our department. Our own motivation is. We must deal with the conflict of our own motivations. Paul instructs them, "Do nothing from selfish ambition or conceit, but in humility count others more significant that yourselves. Let each of you look not only to his own interests, but also to the interests of others" (Philippians 2:3–4). Not a single one of us can rightly judge the motives of another heart. It is not our place and, frankly, not our responsibility.

Our responsibility is to preach the gospel, to share with a lost and dying world the good news of Jesus Christ. Our ultimate interest in others should be the salvation of their souls.

Sometimes I think my motivation is pure. I think my heart's desire is to see God glorified. I think I truly love the people to whom I am ministering. And then I don't get a thank-you. Or compliments. Or accolades. Or someone else receives them. That sting I feel reveals a lot about my true motivation. My selfish ambition for praise and recognition rears its ugly head. I repent of my selfish ambition. Again. I repent of my conceit. Again. I repent of thinking of my own importance. Again.

These brothers Paul is talking about probably have a wide variety of motives. We do not know the reasons they were preaching out of envy and rivalry. Maybe they thought they could have a bigger church or more followers and that would bother Paul. Maybe their motives looked very similar to our own; perhaps they sought praise or accolades or financial gain.

We do know there were those who preached the gospel out of love, who were encouraged to be bold by Paul's imprisonment. Hopefully, we can learn from these faithful followers to adopt similar motives.

Contentment in this conflict comes from reminding ourselves that God knows our vain tendencies. God knows our desires for His glory, both as thieves of glory and as those who want to glorify Him at the same time. God knows. And His grace covers it. He gently reveals the inner workings of our hearts. He gently calls us to repent. He readjusts our motives again and again.

Contentment in this conflict resides in the fact that God's message of salvation is greater than motives. We can rejoice when we hear the true gospel being proclaimed as Paul did. We can trust God to sort out the motives of others as Paul did. We can share the gospel out of love, keeping our own motives in check by faithfully looking to the interests of others, doing nothing out of vain ambition or conceit.

TWENTY-TWO

Those Who Leave the Church

ALMOST EVERY YEAR the results of a survey get published on the beliefs and practices of those who claim to be Christians. The results of these studies show an increasing disparity between the number who claim faith in Christ and those who know the teachings of Christ. It makes sense that if the majority of people in our churches and in greater society claim to be Christians but do not know or practice the basic tenets of the faith, eventually they will leave the faith. Paul writes to the Philippians, "Brothers, join in imitating me, and keep your eyes on those who walk according to the example you have in us. For many, of whom I have often told you and now tell you even with tears, walk as enemies of the cross of Christ. Their end is destruction, their god is their belly, and they glory in their shame, with minds set on earthly things" (Philippians 3:17–19). There are many reasons people attend church and profess Christ when they do not truly believe. But in the end, the reasons aren't important for the purpose we are addressing. At some point, they walk away.

Paul encountered this with one of his companions. In Philemon, he sends greetings from Demas, listing him among "my fellow workers." In Colossians 4:14, Paul sends greetings from Demas as well. But something happens between these letters and the second letter to Timothy. "For Demas, in love with this present world, has deserted me and gone to Thessalonica" (2 Timothy 4:10).

Paul warns Timothy in his first letter that some will "depart from the faith by devoting themselves to deceitful spirits and the teachings of demons, through the insincerity of liars whose consciences are seared" (1 Timothy 4:1–2).

Jesus spoke in parables about those who would fall away. He says there will be the one who "immediately receives [the word] with joy, yet has no root in himself, but endures for a while, and when tribulation or persecution arises on account of the word, immediately he falls away" (Matthew 13:20–21). There will be those in whom "the cares of the world and the deceitfulness of riches choke the word, and it proves unfruitful" (Matthew 13:22). In short, they love something else more than they love Christ.

Absolutely everything we have discussed so far points to consciously choosing to love God more than anything else. Loving God, being wholly satisfied in Him, enjoying His gifts without desiring them, being wholeheartedly devoted in pursuing deep satisfaction with Him are safeguards against walking away. Do you see how those who are truly in Christ are going to continue in their walk because He is everything to them? Paul tells the Philippians,

"But our citizenship is in heaven, and from it we await a Savior, the Lord Jesus Christ, who will transform our lowly body to be like his glorious body, by the power that enables him even to subject all things to himself. Therefore, my brothers, whom I love and long for, my joy and crown, stand firm thus in the Lord, my beloved" (Philippians 3:20–4:1). We must stand firm. We must take care that our affections are solely fixed on Christ. Our citizenship is in heaven. Our submission is to our King. Our hope is our transformation.

But what about those who walk away? To be certain, we now have conflict with them because, as Paul puts it, they are enemies of the cross. At first read, this may seem harsh. I mean, "enemies"?

Think about it this way: by walking away from Christ, they are saying there is something better than Him. There is something they would rather participate in than fellowship with Him. Their evil passions are better. Their worldly pursuits are better.

Worse, think how they speak of their abandonment. Most don't say, "I was walking as a Christian, but I fell in love with the world and abandoned Christ." No. Most say, "I tried that for a while, but it was too rigid. I tried Christianity and it didn't work. The church was full of hypocrites. I couldn't follow all the rules. I got tired of everyone judging me." This kind of language paints a picture in which they believe the error belongs to the church itself or to the doctrines and practices of the faith. They bear witness through speech and action to this errant belief, making themselves an enemy of the cross.

Judas, who walked with Christ during His earthly ministry, was indistinguishable from the other disciples. We begin to see—toward the end—that Judas was a man motivated by riches. He chastised the woman who poured out the jar of perfume because he claimed it could be used for the poor while his own hand was in the moneybag (John 12:1–7). He betrayed Jesus for thirty pieces of silver. He deemed a bag of coins to be better than his friend and Rabbi.

Even more dangerous are those not in the faith who stay in the church. The entire book of Jude paints a picture of insolent, rebellious, sensuous people walking among the saints, eating at the table of Christ, fellowshipping with the believers, while disbelieving the gospel. They are scoffers, following their worldly passions, devoid of the Spirit, ultimately causing divisions.

Paul warns Timothy about the "lovers of self, lovers of money, proud, arrogant, abusive, disobedient to their parents, ungrateful, unholy, heartless, unappeasable, slanderous, without self-control, brutal, not loving good, treacherous, reckless, swollen with conceit, lovers of pleasure rather than lovers of God, *having the appearance of godliness,* but denying its power" (2 Timothy 3:1–7, emphasis added). These people will appear to be walking in the truth of the gospel, but they are not transformed by its power. They are walking in the flesh. They will seek to lead others astray.

Peter cautions, "But false prophets also arose among the people, just as there will be false teachers among you, who will secretly bring in destructive heresies, even denying the Master who bought them, bringing upon themselves swift destruction. And many will follow their sensuality, and because of them the way of truth will be blasphemed. And in their greed they will exploit you with false words" (2 Peter 2:1–3). They "count it pleasure to revel in the daytime. They are blots and blemishes, reveling in their deceptions, while they feast with you. They have eyes full of adultery, insatiable for sin. They entice unsteady souls. They have hearts trained in greed. Accursed children! Forsaking the right way, they have gone astray" (2 Peter 2:13–15). All of 2 Peter 2 serves as a grim warning.

People who are *in* the church but not *of* the church are not satisfied to walk in their disbelief alone. They want to bring others along. They stir up divisions, they corrupt the thinking of others, they lead others along a path of sensuality and sin. Paul says these divisions and factions are necessary to show who is a genuine believer (1 Corinthians 11:17–19).

In this area of conflict, contentment serves us as a keeper and protector. Contentment keeps us from straying after the empty promises greed offers. If we are content with what we have, monetarily speaking, we are less likely to seek ungodly gain. If we are content in our marriage or singlehood, we are less likely to be seduced by adulterers and sensuality. If we are content with our circumstances, we are less likely to be swayed by the promises of easy ways out. If we are content with our Master, we are less likely to follow blasphemies that would deny His power over our lives.

Focus your attention on your eternal citizenship and your coming King.

How do we handle the conflict of those who leave?

Treat them as an unbeliever. Love them. Share the gospel with them. Walk with them in their fear of persecution or troubles of this world. Minister to them.

Have mercy on them. Jude teaches, "And have mercy on those who doubt; save others by snatching them out of the fire; to others show mercy with fear, hating even the garment stained by flesh" (Jude 1:22–23). You who have been shown tremendous mercy, who have been snatched from the fire of hell, who have had your stained garments traded for robes of righteousness—you show mercy to others.

Some who appear to have walked away are doubting. They need mercy. Some who appear to have walked away are hurting. They need mercy. Some who appear to have walked away, well, have walked away. They need mercy. Some who appear to be godly have walked away in their hearts. You guessed it: they need mercy too. Stand firm in your beliefs. Love them as they struggle with theirs.

John reminds us in his first letter that those who go out from among us are not always *of us*; that is, they were perhaps not believers (1 John 2:19). They need the gospel. They need to be told, with love, the truth in which we believe.

Be diligent in guarding your walk. Peter reminds his readers that the day of the Lord is coming, and His patience gives opportunities for repentance. God's "slowness" in returning means patience toward us—and those who stray—saving us from the fate of perishing. He urges us to "be diligent to be found by him without spot or blemish, and at peace" (2 Peter 3:14). He reminds us that knowing there are false teachers among us prepares us. "You, therefore, beloved, knowing this beforehand, take care that you are not carried away with the error of lawless people and lose your own stability. But grow in the grace and knowledge of our Lord and Savior Jesus Christ" (2 Peter 3:17–18).

TWENTY-THREE

Those Who Disagree within the Church

I AM GOING to say it again: conflict stinks.

And yet, conflict happens. In the church conflict happens a lot. And "conflict resolution" doesn't. Not often, and not well.

Paul writes to the Philippians, "I entreat Euodia and I entreat Syntyche to agree in the Lord. Yes, I ask you also, true companion, help these women, who have labored side by side with me in the gospel together with Clement and the rest of my fellow workers, whose names are in the book of life" (Philippians 4:2–3).

Paul gives a lot of shout-outs in his letters. This is not one I would like to receive. Can you imagine having your name forever associated with a church spat? Since I do not like spats at all, this would be a nightmare for me. And yet, this type of conflict is what we are most likely to encounter.

Paul speaks personally to each woman. Paul entreats them to get along. He urges, beseeches, implores, pleads with them to agree in the Lord. He asks his true companion (we do not know who this is) to help them. He calls upon Clement and the other colaborers as well.

Since we do not know if this was a one-time argument that led to a rift or an ongoing contentious relationship, we can address both.

In the case of a one-time argument, Jesus gives two sets of instructions: If your brother has something against you, go to him. If your brother has sinned against you, go to him. Jesus emphasizes this as so urgent, you are to leave your offering at the altar and go take care of it. Seek restoration. Seek forgiveness and give forgiveness (Matthew 5:23–24; 18:15).

Forgiveness is the beauty of the church. We are a forgiven people. Jesus ties our forgiven status to our forgiveness of others throughout the gospels. Why? Though justified in God's sight—we stand before Him with a clean record—here on Earth, we have stained records. We have sinned against our fellow man. We will intentionally and unintentionally be selfish and prideful; we will wound; we will hurt feelings and inflict pain. We will react in anger when we should respond in love. We will seek our own good when we should seek the good of the church. We will become obsessed with the specks in others' eyes while we ignore the planks in our own.

And so, again and again—and again—we seek forgiveness and reconciliation. Reconciliation is putting the relationship back to the way it was, renewing the fellowship. I am convicted of my own tendency to "forgive" yet want nothing whatsoever to do with that person ever again. I am convicted of my tendency to forgive and keep the offender at a distance. Jesus says, "Be reconciled."

Our contentment is on the line. We cannot be at peace with God if we continue in unforgiveness and unreconciled relationships with our brothers. We are violating God's Word to do so.

We need to make a monumental adjustment within our churches as to how we address conflict. From the pastor down, we need to create a culture where we lovingly confront sin, yet graciously and lovingly tolerate differences of opinion or personality.

My gut reaction when someone brings my sin to my attention is to think, "Who do you think you are?! I can point out your sin just as easily!" Through the grace of God, I am learning to say, "I take this very seriously. Could we sit down and talk about this?" If the person is willing to meet with me, to show me biblically where I am erring, I have a true friend who cares about my soul. If they are not willing, there is likely something unrelated going on. But I listen. And pray about what they said.

Is it comfortable? Not at all. Is it easy? Having your sin addressed never is.

The other side of that coin is this: make sure you are actually addressing sin. Be willing to sit down and explain biblically what you are concerned with. Speak the truth in love. Let your conversation be seasoned with salt. Focus on the goal of building up your listener into spiritual maturity. Do not confront in anger. Check your motives: are you offended because your personal preference was violated or your perceived authority was challenged? Is it really, truly sin that needs to be addressed, or were your feelings hurt?

Is your goal reconciliation? Are you willing to engage in relationship to walk with this person as they overcome this sin? Are you willing to love this fellow sinner extravagantly? If you love them enough to point out their sin, do you love them enough to keep the matter between yourselves? If you are not, then you are not permitted to say one word about their sin to them.

I will say this again—and one hundred more times if necessary—we are not to confront on issues of preference, personality differences, or perceived offense to ourselves or others. Jesus said, "when your brother has sinned against you," not "when your brother ruffles your feathers" or "rubs you the wrong way." I have never seen actual statistics on the matter, but most church conflict falls under the ruffled feathers category. The solution for personality or preference-based conflict is self-examination (what does this person reveal about me that I don't like?), prayer, time with that person, and serving toward the common goal of the gospel.

As you grow in contentment, you will grow in your ability to accept the humanity of others. I have learned that most of what bothers me in other people is just their humanness. It is just the little things that make them frail, fallible, faulty people.

As we grow in peace and stillness in the Lord, the little things other people do will matter less. We can embrace them as they are without feeling the need to "fix" anything about them. Not every matter needs to be confronted. The Holy Spirit does a great job of bringing areas of growth to our attention, so we should leave that to Him as much as possible.

"Above all, keep loving one another earnestly, since love covers a multitude of sins" (1 Peter 4:8). First, love keeps the matter covered, as in not on display or disclosed to others, only between the parties involved. We love well when we keep matters of offense to ourselves. Love covers the sin as well when we recognize that we are all works in progress. We can cover someone's offense with our love by praying for them, reaching out to them to build a loving relationship, encouraging them in their walk, and in humility being transparent about the grace and mercy we have received to overcome sin and temptations.

Paul was calling upon his fellow workers to help these women. For the sake of unity in the church, sometimes this is necessary, and again, it should be handled with grace and mercy. Jesus instructed, after going to your brother who has sinned against you, "if he does not listen, take one or two others along with you, that every charge may be established by the evidence of two or three witnesses" (Matthew 18:16). The rest of Matthew 18 outlines how to address church discipline. This is a matter to be taken with the utmost care and concern. This is serious business. This should be reserved for matters of true sin, not trivial offenses. Stealing. Adultery. Abuse. Drunkenness. Lying. Blasphemy. How about in the case of Euodia and Syntyche? Chronic ill will? Discord? Strife? Divisive behavior?

Jesus outlines the process of removing an unrepentant brother or sister from the fellowship. They are to be treated as an outsider—one who needs the gospel—not as a brother or sister in Christ. This matter is to be established with two or three witnesses, because, as Jesus says, "If two of you agree on earth about anything they ask, it will be done for them by my Father in heaven. For where two or three are gathered in my name, there am I among them" (Matthew 18:19–20). We are making decisions regarding church discipline as if Jesus Himself were right there among us. Beloved, we should take this very seriously.

Our modern churches tend to err too far on one side or the other. We either turn a blind eye to rampant sin in our midst or confront offenders in anger without grace. We need to weigh deliberately the binding and loosing we are doing in our churches.

Sin is serious business. And so is conflict (and both stink!). We need to seek the Lord's wisdom to handle both well. What joy to reconcile with a brother or sister who was separated from you by sin, whether yours or his. What joy to put differences aside and serve the gospel together. What joy there is in loving—and forgiving—well. Earnestly. Extravagantly. Mercifully.

As we look to Paul, he was able to manage conflict with grace and dignity because he maintained a high view of God and an accurate view of himself. He knew the God He worshipped. He knew His power, majesty, might, and authority. Paul could trust God to protect him when he was persecuted because he knew nothing could touch him if God did not allow it. These persecutors had no power over him. They could break and bruise his body, but they could not take his life if the Lord had not ordained it.

Paul had a solid grasp on his identity. As you read the book of Acts and his letters, you see a well-trained, highly educated man who knew he was redeemed by the grace of God and set apart for a specific purpose. He was aware of the authority he had, but repeatedly reminds his readers that the authority came from God's will. He is honest about the deeds he participated in before Christ intervened in his life. There is a sense of acceptance in Paul's writings of the totality of himself as God's instrument for a chosen mission. The backbone of Paul's identity can be found "in Him"—in Christ—in being created and recreated in Christ for God's glory.

Our ability to handle conflict well must come from the same source. As we face those who oppose or pervert the gospel, those who preach for selfish gain, those who walk away from the church and any disagreements in the church, in the same confidence in God and honest sense of identity that Paul had. We can remain humble, remembering our participation in the gospel is an act of divine grace and mercy, not a work of our own genius. We must hold fast to our identity in Him, knowing everything about ourselves and our story have been crafted by God on purpose. When we accept ourselves, we are then able to accept others and their story with grace and dignity.

We can face the taunts or outright persecution of those who are not in Him because they can do nothing to alter our identity in Christ. We can stand up for the truth and purity of the gospel because we know the pure and true gospel is where salvation is found. We can love those who walk away or doubt because we can understand their hurts, doubts, fears, and struggles. We can love them genuinely, without making returning a condition of friendship. We can genuinely accept them, where they are in their journey, loving them as they are at any given moment.

It is the rich variance of personality, temperament, goals, gifts, visions, and passions that make the church the beautiful body she is. If the church were made up clones of myself, there is a lot that would never get done. We might have great dinners and long talks, but the church financial accounts would be a mess. We might have great potlucks and Bible studies, but you wouldn't see a business meeting, church workday, or strategy planning. A church entirely made up of people like me would not last long!

Because we are so varied—and so human—conflict within the church is inevitable. Because the church is to be different from the world, conflict with those outside the church is inevitable. God allows the conflict to occur to refine us and grow us. I still think conflict stinks, but the fruit of reconciliation, forgiveness, and unity despite differences is spectacular!

As I have pursued contentment, I have found an increasing awe of God's power over creation. I am learning to rely on the sufficiency of God as the Creator and Sustainer of all. I am learning that this power is the source of contentment in conflict.

God has created me. I know I am a mixed bag of personality, hopes, dreams, defeats, successes, experiences, quirks, and habits. I can see how God has written my story with all its twists and turns that have made me who I am today. I accept the difficult parts of my story because they have shaped me. I accept the beautiful parts of my story because they are the color and joy of my journey. I am not one-dimensional. I am complex. I am still "under construction."

He has created every person I will ever face conflict with. Each and every one of them is an image bearer of the holy, almighty God.

He created them with quirks and different ways of looking at the world. By keeping in mind our status as "in progress" (that is, saved but not yet made perfect), we can recognize this in others and cover their offenses with love. If we are both in the Lord, we can more easily work to agree in the Lord when we remember His great love for the other. My role is to be a respecter of creation, not a subcontractor in the work He is doing.

God is actively at work recreating us. Just as He sustains the universe by the might of His power, He sustains that which He recreates—the church—perfectly. God's mighty, powerful hand is guarding and keeping the bride until the day she is presented to her Groom. He has proven Himself faithful, even against the most astonishing persecution. He has kept a number of faithful believers. He has done what no human mind can conceive: He uses persecution to grow the church and refine her to complete purity. He has recreated us as His workmanship to do good works in the world, works which He prepared in advance for us.

Just like we can trust the certainty of the sun rising in the morning and setting in the evening, we can trust the plan of reconciliation between believers outlined in Scripture. The same God who calls out the stars by name, night after night, and brings the moon back to full, month after month, is the God who commands us to love one another deeply and sincerely, covering a multitude of sins. If He can be trusted to keep something as mighty and massive as the universe in order, can we not trust Him in how to keep His family in order?

He has laid out His instructions and expectations clearly. Contentment—especially when we are faced with conflict—comes through trusting His instructions for the church He created. Even when we face opposition (from within or without) as we obey our Creator's instructions, we can be at peace. We can be content.

Part Five

CONTENTMENT IN COMMUNITY

TWENTY-FOUR

The Christian Community

PAUL'S WRITINGS have three major themes: right doctrine, right identity, and right living, particularly in the context of the church as a community. Books like Ephesians, Colossians, and 1 and 2 Timothy follow this pattern like an outline. Some of his writings are very heavy in the right doctrine, such as Romans and Galatians, with just a little bit of the other two themes, while the letters to the Corinthians are mostly about right living as a church with little snippets of right doctrine and right identity intermingled. In many of Paul's writings, he builds arguments in regard to right doctrine, then uses "therefore" as the segue to transition to the application.

The book of Philippians is a highly personal letter, where Paul reveals more of his own doctrine, identity, and living, while encouraging the Philippians in these matters. The three themes are woven together throughout the whole book seamlessly; he gives statements and doctrinal statements freely, intermingling them with application, and vice versa.

As we turn to look at Paul's teachings to the Philippians on how to live rightly in the church community, we will also look at some doctrinal statements Paul puts forth as motivation and how they are to shape our identity.

Paul begins his instructions on right living in the passage we looked at in the last section regarding those who oppose the gospel. To be sure, much of our need for right living in community is because of opposition coming from outside the church, from those who wish to see the Christian faith destroyed. Paul tells them, "Only let your manner of life be worthy of the gospel of Christ, so that whether I come and see you or am absent, I may hear of you that you are standing firm in one spirit, with one mind striving side by side for the faith of the gospel, and not frightened in anything by your opponents" (Philippians 1:27–28). We see Paul beginning to shape a picture of what the Christian community looks like.

But first, let's talk about what Paul means when he says, "Let your manner of life be worthy of the gospel of Christ." Most of us view these instructions as if Paul is telling us to figure out how to earn Jesus' sacrifice, to somehow pay Him back for what He did. No! Paul is telling us to live as if the gospel is *worth* living for. Live as if you have found the greatest prize known to man. Live as if you are the beloved of the King of Kings. Live as if you have a magnificent, secure, eternal destination. Live as if the gospel has changed you, and since it is worth more than your words can say, show it with your life.

This phrase of Paul's from the Greek means to "behave as a citizen," recognizing the laws and conducting oneself accordingly. Paul reminds readers later, "Our citizenship is in heaven" (Philippians 3:20). We are to act in a way that demonstrates our confidence in our real citizenship and that shows the high value (and cost) of our citizenship. A Roman citizenship was worth a kingly ransom. With it came privileges and responsibilities. How much more valuable is a heavenly citizenship?

In the above passage, Paul introduces a theme that he will build on for much of the remainder of the letter: one spirit, one mind, one purpose. Unity for the sake of the gospel.

Paul introduces this theme under the threat of impending persecution. He tells the Philippians to "[stand] firm in one spirit" and "with one mind [strive] side by side for the faith of the gospel" (Philippians 1:27). Quite literally, we have all been given one Spirit, and this word is most often translated as the Holy Spirit. When speaking of the spirit within us, it is the rational spirit, the power by which one feels, thinks, wills, decides. Martin Luther says this spirit "is the highest, deepest and noblest part of man. By it he is enabled to lay hold on things incomprehensible, invisible, and eternal. It is, in brief, the dwelling-place of faith and the Word of God."[1]

The "one mind" could also be translated as "one soul." We, as a church—as a body—are to have one soul. Intellectually, that makes sense. Our human bodies have one soul, which guides, moves, and influences our actions. Shouldn't it stand to reason that the one body of Christ be filled with one soul that moves it as well?

Since we, as individuals, have placed our faith in Jesus Christ, we as a church and community are to be motivated by our oneness of faith. Individually and collectively, we stand firm in one faith, one spirit. We decide with our will, our rational mind to stand fast —together.

The picture Paul is painting becomes clear. The church should be unified. Each community should have a oneness of purpose, direction, and steadfastness.

In Romans 15:30, Paul urges his readers (and all of us) to "strive together." Interestingly, the only other time the word *strive* gets used in the New Testament is in Philippians 4:3, where the ESV translates it as "labored" together, or "side by side with me." Paul is stating explicitly that the church community should be *working* together. Part of right living is striving together for the gospel. We should all be working as diligently and faithfully as Paul himself labored. He should be the rule, not the exception.

In urging Euodia and Syntyche to reconcile, he was urging them to come back to one mind. To agree in the Lord. He was reminding them—as he reminds the whole church—that our agreement is found in one mind, one spirit, one purpose in the gospel. The language of the two exhortations is mirrored. Behave as a citizen of heaven (Philippians 1:27); our citizenship is in heaven (Philippians 3:20). He wanted to hear that his readers were of one spirit with one mind laboring for the gospel (Philippians 1:27), and he entreated Euodia and Syntyche to agree, be of one mind, in the

Lord because they had labored together with Paul for the gospel (Philippians 4:3).

Paul expounds on this theme in Philippians 2:1–2: "So if there is any encouragement in Christ, any comfort from love, any participation in the Spirit, any affection and sympathy, complete my joy by being of the same mind, having the same love, being in full accord and of one mind."

Is there any encouragement in Christ? Or comfort from love? Participation in the Spirit? Affection or sympathy? If so, then we are to be of the same mind, have the same love, be in full accord, and have one mind. The "if" Paul uses here is not a conditional phrase such as, "If it rains, I will bring my umbrella" but more of a "since" type of terminology: "Since it is raining, I brought my umbrella." Since you are in Christ, since you all are in Christ, you have all these at your disposal; therefore, act in unity.

It is fascinating to watch the differences in churches that have a one-mind mentality versus those with an "every man for himself" attitude. Of course, every individual comes into the church with a distinct personality, a unique combination of strengths and weaknesses, talents, abilities, giftings, and passions. In a one-mind church, this flows into a synergistic expression of God's redemptive work. The church begins to strive together for the gospel in a way where one person's weaknesses are helped by another person's strengths; a passion in one area gives fire for another passion to launch; one dream gives a platform for another's service. Each individual works within the way God created them, making it possible for them together to do more than any could do on their own.

In the self-driven church, each person fights for their dream; each territory is marked by individual blood, sweat, and tears; time, attention, and resources are fought over like scraps thrown to a hungry pack of dogs; other members are only as useful for fueling the mission of self. Little gets done for the gospel since each member is busy striving for their own passion.

Paul makes it clear that we have individual responsibility for a corporate atmosphere. And Paul makes it clear that there is no such thing as an inactive member of a congregation, just as there are no inactive parts of a human body (1 Corinthians 12).

Paul tells them what that mind should look like:

> Do nothing from selfish ambition or conceit, but in humility count others more significant than yourselves. Let each of you look not only to your own interests, but also to the interests of others. Have this mind among yourselves, which is yours in Christ Jesus, who, though he was in the form of God did not count equality with God a thing to be grasped, but emptied himself, by taking the form a servant, being born in the likeness of men. And being found in human form, he humbled himself by becoming obedient to the point of death, even death on a cross. (Philippians 2:3–8)

In this doctrinal statement about Christ, Paul also shows how we are to live. Our minds are to be the same as Christ's—because we already have it, the mind of humility.

I want to tell you a little story from history. There was once a man name Philip. Philip was a king; his official title was King Philip II of Macedon. He was a great military ruler and conquered a city known as Crenides, which he renamed in honor of himself: Philippi. Like most Greek kings of the time, Philip was insatiable in his conquest for more: more land, more power, more wealth, and more honor. Philippi was strategically located on an east-west route through the area that would become his kingdom. It was surrounded by gold mines. Philip established this city that would later become known as "little Rome," complete with theaters, colonnades, baths, forums, and temples.

Philip was by all accounts a self-assured, confident hero of a king. Philip had such brazen confidence that he created a temple of sorts to his own honor. Called the Philippeion, it was a circular memorial, the only one in ancient Greece dedicated to a human. By fashioning himself and his family in statues of ivory and gold, Philip was in essence declaring his godhood. There are also accounts of a procession of gold deities being brought into the city, followed by a golden replica of King Philip.[2]

This was a man who was making himself after the likeness of a god.

Paul writes about God who made Himself after the likeness of man. A man who was a servant. A man who was obedient, even to death. This man was humiliated, scorned, mocked, rejected, and still served us in His death on the cross.

In our flesh, we are more prone to be like King Philip than King Jesus. We exalt ourselves in our victories and claim authority over our places of "service," treating them like cities we have conquered. Rather than exalt our King with the mind He has given us, we ask others to bow to our whims and dreams.

Philip exalted himself, though his kingship was short-lived. Monuments and cities may bear his name, but his reign ended through assassination. His son, Alexander the Great, created a vast empire. But his reign was short-lived as well, dying after just thirteen years on the throne. Jesus alone reigns permanently. "Therefore God has highly exalted him and bestowed on him the name that is above every name, so that at the name of Jesus every knee should bow, in heaven and on earth and under the earth, and every tongue confess that Jesus Christ is Lord, to the glory of God the Father" (Philippians 2:9–11).

Brothers and sisters, we bear the name Jesus. We bear the mind of Jesus. Our humility and unity should bear witness that we have bent the knee to this King. We do not serve ourselves and our ambition, but rather the highly exalted risen Savior and the good news of the salvation He brings.

Jesus is the ultimate example of doing nothing out of selfish ambition or vain conceit. Though God, He died so that you and I could be counted children of God. He thought of the glory of God the Father. He endured the death of the Roman cross with others in mind.

Paul urges his readers to do nothing for selfish reasons. We, however, are terribly prone to selfish reasons. We must continually turn our attention back to Christ's example. Paul teaches that Christ's humility is ours because we have been supernaturally endowed through the power of the Holy Spirit to think like Jesus.

This otherworldly humility is ours because God has placed us under Christ's authority.

Contentment fuels and enables true humility and healthy church community relationships. When we are satisfied with God, fully at peace with Him, growing in our trust of His sovereignty and provision in our lives, we can live in community with others without seeking fulfillment through them. We can live in a community of growth and mutual edification because we aren't seeking from others what can only be found in Christ. The body can live as a functioning whole with Christ as the head. We can gain strength and encouragement from the body without being demanding.

Christian community is where we prove our contentment. Our hearts will be exposed through our interactions with other believers. Let us grow into communities of faith where we seek contentment and demonstrate it through willing service. Let us be individuals whose contentment impacts our community, not the other way around.

TWENTY-FIVE

Three Examples

PAUL GIVES three examples of the type of humility he instructed the Philippians to adopt. We are going to start with his third example: Epaphroditus.

Epaphroditus had come from Philippi to deliver gifts from the church to Paul (Philippians 4:18). While visiting Paul, the man fell ill. Very ill. Epaphroditus almost died. Paul writes,

> I have thought it necessary to send you Epaphroditus my brother and fellow worker and fellow soldier, and your messenger and minister to my need, for he has been longing for you all and has been distressed because you heard that he was ill. Indeed he was ill, near to death. But God had mercy on him, and not only on him but on me also, lest I should have sorrow upon sorrow. I am the more eager to send him, therefore, that you may rejoice at seeing him again, and that I may be less anxious. So receive him in the Lord with all joy, and honor such men, for he nearly died for the work of Christ, risking his life to complete what was lacking in your service to me. (Philippians 2:25–30)

Paul clearly loves this man who brought news and a gift from

Philippi, this fellow worker and soldier in the faith. He honors this man who nearly died for the work of Christ. He holds up Epaphroditus as an example of one who counted others as more significant than himself. Epaphroditus counted Paul as more significant because he delivered the gifts, taking upon himself the risks and inconveniences of travel at that time. Epaphroditus was distressed because of the Philippians' reaction to his illness, not over his own illness.

Epaphroditus risked his life to complete what was lacking in their service to Paul. They had prayed for Paul and gathered gifts. What was lacking? A messenger. A gift without delivery is just a nice thought. There was no Western Union® or Venmo®. You couldn't drop a check in the mail and trust the postal service to deliver it. A gift had to be hand delivered. It seems Epaphroditus was pleased to have fulfilled this role as Paul calls him "your messenger and minister to my need." He was not just a hired messenger. He was a minister. He exhibited his selflessness in ministry by providing this service to the church and to Paul.

The second example Paul gives is Timothy.

> I hope in the Lord Jesus to send Timothy to you soon, so that I too may be cheered by news of you. For I have no one like him, who will be genuinely concerned for your welfare. For they all seek their own interests, not those of Jesus Christ. But you know Timothy's proven worth, how as a son with a father he has served with me in the gospel. I hope therefore to send him just as soon as I see how it will go with me, and I trust in the Lord that shortly I myself will come also. (Philippians 2:19–24)

Paul describes two types of people in this paragraph: those who seek their own interests and Timothy. He does not seek his own interests, but those of Jesus Christ. Timothy is a person who demonstrates genuine concern for others.

Paul and Timothy have a special relationship. Timothy was a young man, whose mother, Eunice, was a Jewish Christian and whose father was a Greek. Timothy became a follower of Christ at a young age. According to 2 Timothy 1:5, his grandmother Lois also was a believer. Timothy joins Paul in missionary work in Acts 16. This is the chapter where Paul travels to Philippi in Macedonia, so the Philippians would have been well acquainted with this young minister. He reminds them that they know Timothy's proven worth, his reputation as a faithful minister, a servant of Paul and the gospel.

If you look at the greeting section of Paul's letters—both introduction and closing—you will see that Timothy is listed frequently. Philippians 1:1 says, "Paul and Timothy, servants of Christ Jesus," by way of introduction. Paul calls Timothy his beloved child, his true child in the faith.

Paul gives us Timothy as an example of Christlike humility as well. While the Philippian church knew him personally, we only know his proven worth through the pages of Scripture. We can learn to follow his example. We can likewise become genuinely concerned with the welfare of others. We can learn to seek the interests of Christ Jesus by loving His church well.

The final example we will look at is Paul. He tells the Philippians how he viewed his own life: "Even if I am to be poured out as a drink offering upon the sacrificial offering of your faith, I am glad and rejoice with you all. Likewise, you also should be glad and rejoice with me" (Philippians 2:17–18).

Paul had labored much for the Philippians and wanted to know that he did not labor in vain (Philippians 2:16). Paul calls these loved ones his joy and his crown. They are the reward he will receive from the Lord.

Paul had devoted his life to the gospel. This man was purposeful. Dedicated. Steadfast. Driven. From the moment of his conversion, all we see in him is a desire to know Christ and make Christ known.

Why do we think Paul is exceptional? Shouldn't we all be like Paul? Shouldn't we all be as driven and focused as Paul? We may not all be appointed to go on epic world-wandering missionary journeys. But how would the world be changed if we were all as steadfastly devoted to Jesus as Paul was? If we were all singularly focused on bringing as many into the kingdom as he was? If *nothing*—not even stoning, beatings, death threats, shipwrecks—could stop us from sharing the gospel?

Paul uses an interesting Old Testament reference: the drink offering. Under the Law, each offering was to be accompanied by "a fourth of a hin of wine for a drink offering" (Exodus 29:40). In the instructions for the Tabernacle, Moses was instructed to make flagons and bowls of pure gold, from which to pour out the drink offerings (Exodus 25:29). The wine was to be poured out in the Holy Place (Numbers 28:7). If wine is poured on the fire where an offering is burning, the alcohol will light quickly, and the wine will be consumed.

Paul held nothing back. Paul saw his life as an offering to be consumed. Paul told the Philippians he was "glad" and "rejoiced" to be poured out as a drink offering on the sacrificial offering of their faith (Philippians 2:17) . Later, in his final letter, Paul tells Timothy, "For I am already being poured out as a drink offering, and the time of my departure has come" (2 Timothy 4:6). This is right before he says he fought the good fight and finished the race.

But our churches say, "You can't pour from an empty cup." If you want to know if you should be following an ideology, it is a good idea to see if it is in Scripture. I will save you a step: there is no Bible verse that says you cannot pour from an empty cup.

The modern American church has the struggles it does because we are busier keeping our cups full than we are pouring them out. We pay so much attention to how full we think our cups are that there is little time to devote to pouring out. Unlike Paul, we are fearful or resentful of losing a drop from our cups.

But Paul? He poured out! This is selfless service. This is counting others as more significant than yourselves.

When John Bunyan wrote *The Pilgrim's Progress*, he coined the term *vanity fair*. Literally, it refers to a fair where people went to have their senses indulged. This city, in the allegory, is on the road that Christian takes to the Celestial City. Christian and his companion Faithful pass through the city, and they are treated as alien, with their different clothes and manner of speaking; they disturb the residents because they place so little value on the merchandise being sold. They are scorned and persecuted for not participating in the vain lifestyle of the fair.[1]

Yet the modern church has set up booths at this fair, with loud barkers calling out to fill your cup with whatever it can hold to give you strength to journey on to the Celestial City. You cannot make the journey on an empty cup! Fill, fill, fill!

We have elevated the enjoyment of God's blessings to the same level as the spiritual disciplines. When those in roles of spiritual authority over Christians exalt the practices of self-care as necessity for wholeness in discipleship, the practitioners will frequently equate indulgence of the flesh with spiritual wellness. The spiritual disciplines have become seen as inadequate for wholeness as a believer.

It is time for the church to step back from this ideology and give it a little more consideration. Do not be fooled, dear one, when a covetous culture tells you that you "need" something or that something is for "your good." Even the health and wellness industry—as much as it sounds like these so-called experts care about us, they are making a pretty penny. We need to pause in our headlong rush to follow the leaders of our culture in this pursuit.

This ideology is detrimental to our pursuit of contentment because it tells us there is something other than the Lord we need in order to be whole and well. It is detrimental to our community because it keeps us focused on ourselves, fearful of expending our resources on developing others' faith. It creates classes within the community of those who have the wherewithal to be healthy according to these tenets and those who cannot.

In David's famous Psalm 23, he states, "my cup overflows" (Psalm 23:5). It wasn't because David was filling it. It was because the Lord was his shepherd. Because he had everything he needed in the Lord. The Lord prepared the table before him. The Lord anointed him with oil. The imagery David invokes is of one fat, happy, content sheep, a sheep that trusts fully in the goodness of his shepherd, so he wants for nothing.

The truth is, we do not need to worry about filling our cup (I would mostly fill mine with garbage anyway). We need to look toward emptying it. Being poured out on the sacrificial offering of others. Our church needs it. The world needs it.

When we seek contentment in the Lord, we can take care of ourselves and enjoy the blessings God has given us without becoming self-indulgent. We can delight in the Lord, confident that He will give us each day what we need to live as drink offerings being poured out for others. Enjoy what God gives you as the blessing it is, made holy with prayer and thanksgiving. But enjoy God more.

There is not enough dark chocolate, wine, yoga, sleep, meditation, beach time, girls' nights out, or whatever, to fill a heart that is not satisfied with God and God alone. You cannot turn something God meant for you to enjoy into medication for your sick heart. You cannot obtain spiritual health through indulgence.

Jeremiah Burroughs addressed this in the seventeenth century. He tells of a famished man turning his face to the wind to eat his fill of the wind. This man thought he was still hungry because he had not had enough wind, when the reality is, wind was not made to satisfy the stomach. As Burroughs explains, "Truly there is the same madness in the world; the wind that a man takes in by gaping will as soon satisfy a craving stomach which is ready to famish, as all the comforts in the world can satisfy a soul that knows what true happiness means."[2]

Burroughs proposes that our immortal souls were made for more than the world has to offer. By filling ourselves with merely worldly pleasures, we will always be dissatisfied because we were made to be satisfied with God Himself. Conversely, the more we are filled with God, the more vain we see the pursuits of the world to be.

Being poured out goes against our self-preservation instincts. It goes against our self-indulgent, self-seeking instincts. But this is the call of Christ. When He called you, He called you to die to self. He called you to lay down your rights and your authority over your own life. He also told you that the one who seeks to save their life loses it, but the one who gives it away is the one who finds it.

Do we trust the almighty God of the universe to provide the strength we need for each task He assigns? Do we trust Him to provide the emotional, physical, and spiritual resources to face what He appoints to us as individuals and churches? Do we trust that pouring out ourselves for the sake of the kingdom is worth it?

One of the arguments for focusing on our own cup is, "How can you love your neighbor if you aren't intentional about loving yourself first?" The problem is not a lack of love for ourselves. We love ourselves above all else. The problem is we do not take the first part of Jesus' command seriously, "You shall love the Lord your God with all your heart and with all your soul and with all your soul and with all your mind" (Matthew 22:37). Loving God well edges out our love for self and enables us to love our neighbor well. This love for God keeps our neighbor and ourselves from taking the preeminent place in our hearts. Our love for God and the love we receive from Him become our motivation to pour ourselves out for our neighbor (Matthew 22:36–40).

Jesus commanded His followers to deny self, take up their cross, and follow Him (Matthew 16:24). I have heard this "deny self" part explained away more times than I can count. Our natural inclination would tell us to edit the above verses to read "Love your . . . self" because that sounds better to our selfish hearts than bearing a cross and denying ourselves. It is uncomfortable to make sacrifices for the sake of our Lord. It is difficult to lay aside our rights, ambitions, comforts, or pleasures for others. We have a choice to make: follow Him and deny self, or follow self and deny Him. We cannot do both.

Growing in our complete satisfaction in God and God alone safeguards us against the temptation to pour ourselves out for our own glory and recognition, or an unhealthy sense of people-pleasing. We should not be the ones on every church committee complaining about what a burden it is. We should not sacrifice health and well-being, hoping someone will notice. We should serve out of completion, not neediness. We must learn to pour ourselves out from a place of contentment, not to obtain fulfillment.

Let us enjoy the gifts God has given us. Let us work heartily at the work God has given us. Let us fear God and keep His commands. Let us strive after things of substance: holiness, righteousness, contentment. Let us rejoice in the goodness of our God and bear witness to His graciousness by pursuing Him, not worldly standards.

We should take care of ourselves as an act of stewardship. We have been given these beautiful, wonderful lives and bodies to be filled with fruitful labor to the Lord. By caring for ourselves, we demonstrate thankfulness for our bodies and good stewardship of the precious gift of life He has blessed us with. We take care of ourselves with healthy food, water, rest, prayer, time in the Word, movement, and interpersonal connections.

It will take time to learn your personal balance between taking care of yourself and pouring yourself out. It will take time to learn the balance between enjoying God's good gifts and self-denial, caring for others and allowing others to care for you. Our Lord Jesus was good at this. He stayed up praying one night after a long day of ministry. Another night, he slept below deck while his disciples tried to navigate the boat across the sea. He fasted for forty days in the wilderness, but He also feasted often. He poured out His blood for us, but He also allowed Mary to pour out her perfume for Him. Jesus enjoyed the bounties of God's goodness without ever indulging sinfully. Be patient with yourself as you learn this balance.

Paul also serves as an example for us as one who steadfastly poured himself out for the sake of the communities he loved. He would encourage us to be glad to be poured out on the offering of others' faith. He would tell us to trust the contents of our cup to the Lord. Timothy and Epaphroditus were men following in Paul's foot-steps. The church needs each member to look to others as more significant than self, making sacrifices for others, being poured out gladly and with rejoicing.

TWENTY-SIX

Community Responsibilities

PAUL GIVES two sets of responsibilities to the church in Philippi. First, he tells them, "Therefore, my beloved, . . . you have always obeyed, so now, not only as in my presence but much more in my absence" (Philippians 2:12).

As Christians, we each have the responsibility to be obedient. Paul gave the Philippians the gospel and instructions for living. They were obedient while he was present and were demonstrating a continued obedience in his absence. This is the model: lifelong obedience. Obedience to the Word of God, to the Holy Spirit within us, and to the leaders God has placed over us. One of the parenting classes we took when we had wee ones defined obedience as "doing what you are told, right away, all the way, and with a good attitude." Trying to teach our children to obey us as earthly parents gave me insight into my own heart. If this standard of obedience is for my children in my earthly commands, what are my excuses for not obeying my heavenly Father with the same standard on eternal matters?

Secondly, Paul then tells them, "Work out your own salvation with fear and trembling" (Philippians 2:12). I think this is one of the coolest verses in the Bible. When I gave you a brief history lesson on

Philippi in chapter 24, I mentioned that the town was known for its gold mines. In fact, the hills surrounding the city were full of them. This "work out" phrase can be used as a mining term. It is a compound word, transliterated *katergazomai*. The second part of the word, *ergazomai*, means work. The first part, *kata*, is a preposition, a directional word, where the "out" part comes from.[1]

Imagine yourself as a mine. Rather than veins of gold, you are filled with veins of righteousness, Christlikeness, holiness. When you received salvation, the mine was filled. Now you must do the work of bringing it from the inside.

Paul is telling us to bring out intentionally the behaviors of the salvation that dwells within us. It goes against our sin nature, our habits, patterns, and behaviors. We may not want to do the things in accordance with the salvation within us, which is why there is an element of "work" to this. It takes no work for sin to bring itself forth from our depths. We must work against it.

I want to illustrate this with an imperfect example: childbirth. Even if you have never given birth to a child, you are probably familiar with how the process works. The woman has a child inside her, and she is working to bring the child out. The body, through a complex system of hormones and uterine contractions, works to bring the child out. The mother—through her will—works with her body to bring the child out. The mother has no power over the natural process her body is undergoing through the system God put in place (and doctors can't really explain how it all works either). But as she walks, breathes, rests, and pushes, she partners with her body to accomplish the birth. This is work—aptly named "labor"—and takes considerable effort.

We have this salvation within us. Through the complex system I cannot explain, the Holy Spirit works within us to sanctify and change us. We partner with Him in this process to bring that salvation out into the life we live daily. Just as a woman cannot bring a child into the world if there is no child in her womb (she can walk, breathe, and push all day every day to no avail), we cannot bring forth the behaviors of sanctification if we are not in Christ and indwelt by the Holy Spirit. If we are filled with self, our labor will only give birth to sin.

This all goes back to the word Paul uses in the first line of Philippians 2:12: obey. Obey the commands of Scripture. Our communities would be shaped enormously if we took to heart and obeyed the commands of Scripture. The apostles echo the words Jesus spoke to His followers as recorded in the Gospels: if you love me, you will keep my commands. We are expected to be obedient.

But why does Paul say "with fear and trembling"? Beloved, we must never take the grace of God for granted. We do not have to be afraid of God. But we should fear Him with reverential awe. This is the Almighty. The holy God of the universe. We have become flippant about who God is and have trivialized the significance of what God has done.

You, my dear friend, have the Holy Spirit of God within you. You have the power of creation, the power that rose Jesus from the dead *within you*. We should treat our salvation as the serious indwelling it is. You deserve to be on the receiving end of the wrath of God, not the indwelling, empowering end. You deserve to be cut off and separated from God. You deserve the punishment that all that sin has earned.

The word *trembling*, transliterated *tromos*, throughout Greek writing is "used to describe the anxiety of one who distrusts his ability to meet all requirements, but religiously does his utmost to fulfill his duty."[2] And honestly, we *should* distrust our own ability. We are frightfully prone to sin, with fragile egos and fearful misinterpretations of Scripture. If I had to rely on my own ability to meet the requirements of God, I shudder to think of where I would end up.

I do not have to rely on myself, praise the Lord, Hallelujah! Jesus has fulfilled the duty on my behalf! He has made me His own. Out of love for Him, I am now free to do my utmost religiously to fulfill my duty. I am now able to renounce sin, to walk in love, to be obedient.

Are you religiously doing your utmost? This is the standard, the expectation. This is not for the "super Christians" like Peter and Paul. This is for everyone.

Paul reminds us that, after all, "it is God who works in you, both to will and to work for his good pleasure" (Philippians 2:13). All of this is a work of God. All of it. As I reflect on the definition of contentment I shared in the first chapter from Jeremiah Burroughs, "Freely submitting to and taking complacency in God's disposal," this verse encapsulates his desire.[3] To want only the things that will bring God pleasure. To want only the things that are of God's will for my life. To be "well pleased with God's hand."[4]

As a community, the church has responsibilities as well. For example, as Paul tells the Philippians, "Do all things without grumbling or disputing" (Philippians 2:14).

All things. Without grumbling. Without disputing.

Have you ever been in a church where no one grumbles or disputes? That sounds amazing! We should work toward that end. Perhaps this was Paul's soft warm-up to addressing Euodia and Syntyche later in the letter. We should each, as individuals, address our tendencies to grumble and dispute, but as a church we must also develop an atmosphere where there isn't room for complaining.

Paul gives the reason for being a community without grumbling: "that you may be blameless and innocent, children of God without blemish" (Philippians 2:15). The church bears a lot of blame for how people perceive God. How can the world look at our grumbling and disputing and see a God who is trustworthy, loving, caring, compassionate, or wise? The word *innocent* means free from harm. We certainly do a lot of harm with complaining. We do a lot of harm with grumbling. We do a lot of harm with disputing.

Beloved, this cannot be!

Look at the rest of this verse and the following verse: "without blemish in the midst of a crooked and twisted generation, among whom you shine like lights in the world, holding fast to the word of life, so that in the day of Christ I may be proud that I did not run in vain or labor in vain" (Philippians 2:15–16). We, too, are in the midst of a crooked and twisted generation. Every generation is.

What is our responsibility as a church? To be without blemish, to shine like lights, and to hold fast to the word of life.

The Levitical requirement of all sacrifices was perfection. Every animal presented to God was to be without blemish. No injuries, pimples, scabs, missing parts, etc. This was important in the sacrificial system for many reasons. First, it ensured that God was given the best. If you had a sick animal that you couldn't eat, the temptation to offer it as a sacrifice would be strong. Second, it proved your trust in God. If you gave Him the best of the flock, you had to trust that the rest would be good enough to reproduce and provide food. Third (and most important), it pointed to Christ. Christ, our blameless, perfect sacrifice, was completely without blemish, physically and spiritually.

Christ, as the Lamb of God without any blemish, became our substitution; therefore, we are without blemish. We are made pure. We are made right with God. We are made righteous before God.

We are without blemish in the midst of a twisted and crooked generation. The Greek word for twisted, *skolios*, means "crooked, curved; metaphorically, perverse or wicked" or bent toward evil.[5] The word for crooked, *diastrephō*, means "to distort or misinterpret, to turn aside from the right path, to pervert or corrupt."[6]

The way of the world is to twist and manipulate everything about God to make Him look evil. It corrupts what He says is good. It says what He calls evil is actually good. As individuals and churches, we need to be careful we are not giving the world ammunition. Honestly, it will happen anyway, but we need to watch ourselves.

We are on display. We are the crazy, foolish ones who have given our lives for a God who died and rose again. We turn the other cheek and love our enemies. We lead by serving. To a world that is crooked and twisted, the straight and narrow seems rigid, unloving, boring, unfair, judgmental, or whatever other adjective the world deems most fitting.

When we try to shine but with a grumbling, critical, disputing, complaining attitude, the world sees it. They think, "Why would I want to follow their God? If they are that mean, what must their

God be like?" or "Why would I want to be a child of God when all that family does is complain and fight?" How is it that the crooked and twisted generation can understand what we are saying by our behavior better than we can?

If we are careful to be blameless and harmless, in word and deed, the world will notice. The twisted and crooked generation will see the lights of unblemished men and women in communities that love the Lord and each other well.

If we are deeply satisfied in God, what is there to grumble about? If we are thinking well, praying at all times with thanksgiving, handling conflict well, trusting in the Lord's sovereign providence in all things, I ask again, what is there to complain about? If we trust the people God has put in leadership, if we trust the goodness of the Shepherd, what will we have to dispute each other about? If we are being obedient to Scripture and the leaders God has given us, I think we can agree that grumbling and disputing are unlikely.

This is why we "hold fast to the word of life" (Philippians 2:16). The Word of God changes us from being twisted and crooked like the rest of our generation. The Word of God teaches to think like Christ, to embrace the wisdom of God, to listen to the Holy Spirit sent to guide us and teach us all truth. The Word of God motivates us to be effective and fruitful. The Word of God gives us hope for eternity and strength to endure whatever the generation we live in will throw at us.

It is not our role to straighten the twisted and crooked generation. This world is not yours. You have a heavenly citizenship, remember. You are just visiting here, just passing through. Do not hold fast to the world. Hold fast to God. Expect the generation you live in to be twisted. Expect evil. Expect corruption. Expect the ways of God and His people to be mocked and the things they say to be manipulated or twisted.

This generation will remain twisted and crooked. There is nothing we can do about that. But *individuals* within this generation can find the same blemish-free life you have in Jesus Christ. When we live in holy community with one another, loving God and neighbor well and pouring ourselves out on the sacrifice of others, this is possible. When the church stands firm with one Spirit, one mind, one purpose, when we are not frightened by our opponents, when we shine as lights in front of them, it will get their attention. When we serve others in humility, we preach our suffering servant Savior who loves us and laid down His life for us. When we are obedient, we show that life found in Him is better than the life we left behind. When we radiate contentment, we shine brightly in the dark generation that desperately wants peace and satisfaction.

We, God's chosen race, royal priesthood, holy nation, people for His own possession, are to be proclaiming the excellencies of His mercies (1 Peter 2:9). What is more merciful than a holy God, utterly separate and distinct, calling us out of darkness that we may share in His marvelous light? We are His greatest witness of His holy work.

God's holiness separates Him and defines Him. There is nothing in this world—or of this world—that compares with Him. Everything good and beautiful in this life is just a taste of His greatness. Our distinctiveness as a community comes from our status as children of the Holy God. We—together—are His church. And we—together—are called to be holy as He is holy. We are to be different from the world as individuals who have been made into new creations, but also different as a community of people who draw near to throne of grace.

We must be unequivocally convinced that nothing this world has to offer is better than following the command, "You shall be holy, for I am holy" (1 Peter 1:16). Peter contrasts this holy command with our natural, futile ways inherited from our forefathers. He tells us, as obedient children, not to be conformed to the passions of our former ignorance. Now that we are in Christ, we are to be different. How completely otherworldly to live in oneness of spirit and mind. How peculiar to risk everything for the message of hope or to be poured out on the sacrifice of another's faith. How completely foreign to do everything without grumbling or complaining. How holy to have the mind of the holy Lamb of God, the unblemished sacrifice for our sins, living in us, this mind of selfless servanthood.

Part Six

CONTENTMENT IN COMPLETION

TWENTY-SEVEN

Paul's Desire

YOU MAY HAVE NOTICED I worked backward through the book of Philippians as we discussed contentment. I did this intentionally because I wanted to save the heaviest—and hardest—for last. Paul looked to the future, where he would be in the presence of Christ, made complete through his own physical death and the final resurrection. As I studied Paul's contentment in completion, I realized that I personally would have to work through a lot of the previous themes before I was ready to address this one myself.

Facing the end of our earthly lives is a difficult subject to address. In His Word, God has graciously given us examples to follow as we turn our attention to this subject. While Paul stands out as a New Testament example, Elijah serves as one from the Old Testament. Elijah was one of two individuals in the Bible who left this life by being taken by God rather than by dying (the other being Enoch, as seen in Genesis 5:24). It seems that Elijah knew his time had come. Since the end of his life came in a unique manner, Elijah gives us a glimpse into his attitude.

In 2 Kings 2, we have Elijah's departure story recorded. He tells his successor, Elisha, to stay behind. On three separate legs of the journey, he urges Elisha to stay behind. But Elisha persists in walking with him. Three times, the other prophets ask Elisha, "Do you know that today the LORD will take away your master from over you?" (2 Kings 2:5). And three times Elisha tells them he knows and asks them to keep quiet. Arriving at the Jordan River, Elijah parts the water for them to cross through on dry land. Elijah lets Elisha make one final request of him. Then the Word says, "And as they still went on and talked, behold, chariots of fire and horses of fire separated the two of them. And Elijah went up by a whirlwind into heaven" (2 Kings 2:11).

Elijah, a man just like us, faced his end with calmness and determination. Whereas Elijah faced a whirlwind of fire, I face a whirlwind of emotions. I feel tied to this world, so hints of heartache spring up at the thought of dying.

Not so for Paul. Is it any surprise that the picture of contentment—the man who most fully embodied deep satisfaction in and with God—lived ready to see God face-to-face? Paul writes honestly,

> Yes, and I will rejoice for I know that through your prayers and the help of the Spirit of Jesus Christ this will turn out for my deliverance, as it is my eager expectation and hope that I will not be at all ashamed, but that with full courage now as always Christ will be honored in my body, whether by life or by death. For to me to live is Christ, and to die is gain. If I am to live in the flesh, that means fruitful labor for me. Yet which I shall choose I cannot tell. I am hard pressed between the two. My desire is to depart and be with Christ, for that is far better. But to remain in the flesh is more necessary on your account. Convinced of this, I know that I will remain and continue with you all, for your progress and joy in the faith, so that in me you may have ample cause to glory in Christ Jesus, because of my coming to you again. (Philippians 1:18–26)

Paul eagerly expected deliverance. He knew prison was not his final destination. He knew God would have him freed to continue ministry or God would have him put to death to enter Christ's presence. Paul clearly saw these as the only two options. He wanted to live in a way that honored Christ whether he lived or died. Living meant fruitful labor. Living meant a greater benefit to the people to whom Paul ministered. Death meant the presence of Christ, which is better by far.

Intellectually, we know that heaven awaits. Seeing our Savior face-to-face will be the best moment we have ever experienced. We will have an eternity to relish in His presence. We may say we agree with Paul's sentiment, "My desire is to depart and be with Christ, for that is far better" (Philippians 1:23).

But we are woefully distraught when we think of death—not just our own but that of our loved ones—even with what we know and believe. We are torn between the two, but not in a confident, content way as Paul expressed.

So much of the grasping, clinging, striving to make this life as beautiful as we can comes from the knowledge that one day it will end. But it also comes with a shocking distrust of God's goodness in our real lives hidden in Christ. Anxieties and fears all stem from *that* final anxiety and fear.

Every day, the messages regarding our control over our own mortality bombard us. All day, every day, we receive messages, such as "Do this or else you'll die," in books, magazines, news, and ads. Headlines promise tips that can save our lives and advertise choices we can make to prolong them.

These messages make us forget that the Lord has already numbered our days (Psalm 139:16). We won't get to heaven and be greeted with, "You know, you were supposed to die ten years ago, but all that kale you ate made me powerless to bring you home." Or "What are you doing here? You weren't scheduled to arrive for another twenty years?"

But still, we listen.

As I study Paul's life for the secrets of his contentment, I do not see a man who fears death. I see a man who thinks of himself as already dead. Paul was crucified with Christ. He said of himself, "The life I now live in the flesh I live by faith in the Son of God, who loved me and gave himself for me" (Galatians 2:20). He states that we have "been buried with him in baptism, in which [we] were

179

also raised with him through faith in the powerful working of God who raised him from the dead" (Colossians 2:12), that "those who live might no longer live for themselves but for him who for their sake died and was raised" (2 Corinthians 5:15).

Addressing death does not give us the joy and contentment Paul expresses because we still think of our lives as our own. When I look at my heart's reasons for wanting to stay here, it looks a lot more like a list of reasons to please myself than pleasing my Lord. I have a list of things I want to accomplish or experience. I have things I haven't seen or done. I have pleasures left untasted. I have hopes and dreams yet unfulfilled.

Paul had one purpose: glorifying God and preaching Christ.

Would I be yearning for heaven if every day I poured myself out on the offering of another's faith, if I woke up every morning with a Paul-like attitude that this day was an opportunity for fruitful labor? Would I fall asleep contented that the Lord could take me home while I slept because I had walked so close with Him throughout the day, it would just seem natural to "wake up" in His presence?

This is the true secret to Paul's contentment. He was a man on purpose, a man on mission. He knew his life was a vapor, and he wanted to take as many into the presence of God with him when the vapor evaporated. He wanted to see every seed he planted rooted and established. He wanted the churches he started to grow up into maturity. He wanted to keep going into new territory. He wanted to know Christ and His sufferings. He wanted to be resurrected.

If we, my beloved readers, are going to be content, we must adopt a Paul-like intensity of purpose. Not all of us will be world-gallivanting church planters. That was Paul's area of service. But God has custom made you just as He did Paul. Each of us has a family, friends, or coworkers, and lives in a neighborhood. We each encounter myriad other people in our daily lives. *These* are the people God has custom designed *us* for our own fruitful labor.

We must determine to start each day with the prayer, *Lord, please show me the fruitful labor You have for me today. Since I woke up still in this body, on whose account was it necessary that I remain?*

Paul could have courage in the face of continued imprisonment, dangerous ongoing ministry, or even execution because he knew that all of these were a means of glorifying God. He only wanted Christ honored through his life.

Paul considered the manner of his death as important as the destination; he wanted Christ to be honored. Paul saw death as better. Paul saw death as gain. Paul desired death so that he could be with Christ. Perhaps if we begin to think of how we can honor Christ with our deaths, we would desire it rather than fear it. As John Piper puts it, "If we suffer and die on the Calvary road of obedience with Christ, the cost of following him is not just a *result* of making much of him, but a *means*. Death makes visible where our treasure is. The way we die reveals the worth of Christ in our hearts. Christ will be praised in my death if in my death he is prized above life."[1]

If death reveals where my treasure is, then what I fear in death amplifies that revelation. I most certainly treasure much of this world above my Savior! I ask for grace and mercy to set these earthly longings aside so my desire to depart and be with Christ may grow.

In 2014, Herb Stoneman passed away. You may not have ever heard of Herb, but he was a gracious man of God who faithfully served as a pastor. Through I was unable to attend his funeral in person, I watched portions that were posted on social media. The funeral ended with a baptism. Herb had led one of his nurses to the Lord, and she was baptized at his celebration of life. *That* is dying well! *That* is Paul-like intensity. *That* is the witness of a man who lived every day with a view of fruitful labor.

This is my end goal in seeking contentment. I want to be content not merely to make my life today more pleasant, but so I can live with the end in sight. I can live with my eyes so firmly focused on my eternal destination that the world has little hold on me. Living means fruitful labor. Death means my hidden life revealed.

If you have ever been to a musical, five to ten minutes before the curtains open, the orchestra will begin to play a medley of songs from the upcoming show. While elements of the musical are contained within this prelude, it is not the show itself. Living for this life alone is like picking up your playbill and leaving when the orchestra ends the prelude. This life is just the introduction. This life is just a sampling of what is to come. All the heart-bursting-with-joy moments here are just a foretaste of fullness of joy there. This is worth the work of putting to death that which is earthly in us. If Christ's presence in my life *here* has been joy, peace, satisfaction, and comfort, how much more will it be in a kingdom not tainted by sin and decay? Oh, how my heart should long for this above all else!

Death is the dominion of this world, of sin, the law, and the prince of this age. I serve the One who has defeated death. I am growing to have no fear in death because death has no power over me. I have no fear of judgment because the "me" deserving punishment has already died. I have been crucified, buried, and raised to new life. I can live confidently, knowing that if Christ is in me, though my body will die, my spirit will live because the same Spirit that raised Jesus from the dead lives in me and will raise me (Romans 8:9–11). I can be steadfast and immovable, knowing that I do not labor in vain because death is swallowed up in victory, the victory we have through Jesus Christ our Lord (1 Corinthians 15:54–58). I am free from lifelong slavery to the fear of death because Jesus has defeated the one who had power over death (Hebrews 2:14–15). I have been buried with Him in baptism and given new life with my whole debt canceled and the entire legal code nailed to the cross. I *was* dead and *have been* made alive (Colossians 2:11–15).

I must continue to wrestle with this, preaching the truth to my heart. Not fearing death is a matter of belief. If we persist in fear, we are disbelieving God's promises. If we are to stand confidently on God's word, being content to glorify Him in life or my death, we must wholeheartedly believe His word. He has promised we will not perish but have everlasting life (John 3:16). We must remind our wayward hearts that the One who raised Jesus will also raise us and bring us into His presence (2 Corinthians 4:13–14).

Paul suffered the loss of all things and counted them all as rubbish, "that I may know him and the power of his resurrection, and may share in his sufferings, becoming like him in death, that by any means possible I may attain the resurrection from the dead" (Philippians 3:10–11). Talk about having a one-track mind! To know the power of Christ's resurrection, become like Him in His death, and attain the resurrection from the dead, we must physically die. We cannot be raised again without that step. We cannot become wholly new—transformed—without dying physically.

Paul is clear: we do not belong here. We are headed somewhere else. Paul calls our earthly life a tent—a temporary shelter—while a permanent house is being built for us in the heavens (2 Corinthians 5:1–5). My problem is I am treating *this tent* like my permanent home. I am hanging drywall and making myself at home in this temporary life. I must remind myself daily to "look not to the things that are seen but to the things that are unseen. For the things that are seen are transient, but the things that are unseen are eternal" (2 Corinthians 4:18).

In many ways, the small deaths to self in pursuing contentment will shape us and prepare us for the final death. When we open our tight-fisted grip on the world by letting go of our wants, trusting God with our needs, renewing our minds, living in community with other believers, seeking satisfaction in and with God above all else, we are dying to our flesh daily, little by little. Charles Spurgeon said, "He who learns to die daily while He lives will find no difficulty to breathe out his soul for the last time."[2]

Like Paul, I want to firmly say, "Yes, we are of good courage, and we would rather be away from the body and at home with the Lord. So whether we are at home or away, we make it our aim to please him" (2 Corinthians 5:8–9). He wanted to be with Jesus, but until he got there, he wanted to honor Christ, with boldness and courage, with his life.

There is a sense of never being fully content *in* this life because we are not made *for* this life. As I wrestle my heart into submission to the truth of the gospel, discontentment with this life grows. In 2 Corinthians 5, Paul writes of groaning while in this tent, a groaning for the permanence. I can never be fully content, fully satisfied in God, until I am finally in His presence, my adoption is finalized, and my resurrection is complete. There is a disquieting comfort to know that I am seeking a contentment that will never be actualized in this lifetime; it awakens a yearning for *that* place and *that* presence of God. It is disquieting because my soul was never meant to be comfortable here. It is comforting because I know I am finally learning the true secret of contentment.

TWENTY-EIGHT

Not Yet

PAUL'S HONESTY gives me great comfort. Since most of our teachings on doctrine, Christian living, and our identity in Christ come from Paul, it is easy to look at him as the prime example. He "gets it," so we model our lives and thinking after his teachings. Yet he calls himself the "foremost" sinner (1 Timothy 1:15) and the "least of the apostles" (1 Corinthians 15:9). This is not false humility, but the honest self-assessment of one who has drawn close to Jesus.

In Philippians, he makes one statement that gives me encouragement because of his honesty as well as his advice. He writes,

> Not that I have already obtained this or am already perfect, but I press on to make it my own, because Christ Jesus has made me his own. Brothers, I do not consider that I have made it my own. But one thing I do: forgetting what lies behind and straining forward to what lies ahead, I press on toward the goal for the prize of the upward call of God in Christ Jesus. Let those of us who are mature think this way, and if in anything you think otherwise, God will reveal that also to you. Only let us hold true to what we have attained. (Philippians 3:12–16)

This passage immediately follows Paul's expressed desire to know Christ and the power of His resurrection, to share in His sufferings, becoming like Him in death that he may attain the resurrection from the dead. He states, I want this, but I have not attained it yet.

Paul was aware of his own failings. He fully recognized that any ground he had gained in Christlikeness was because Christ had taken hold of him. In Philippians 3:12, he says, "Christ has made me his own," and a few verses back in Philippians 3:9, he explains, "not having a righteousness of my own that comes from the law, but that which comes through faith in Christ." This gives me comfort because he is *Paul* and he is owning that he has not been made perfect yet. He is not yet fully righteous. He is not perfectly Christ-like yet. Paul is not shrugging his shoulders with a fatalistic "oh well" attitude in this admission, however.

Instead, he says, "But one thing I do . . . ," and then he gives three things he does (Philippians 3:13–14). He forgets what is behind, he strains forward to what lies ahead, and he presses toward the goal for the prize of the upward call of God in Christ Jesus.

Paul often uses racing and competition imagery in his writings because they were familiar to his Greco-Roman audience. This is one of those times. We have all seen the photo-finish races where the winner crosses the line ahead of his competitor by mere means of stretching himself further than his opponent. His feet may be at the same place on the track, but his chest breaks the finish line tape first. He strains to win just a little bit harder.

Paul mastered his mind to leave the past in the past. He mastered his mind to focus on his eternal destination. He mastered his mind to focus on the prize—being called up to God's presence— the mark at the end of the race.

He then encourages us to think likewise. He calls all who may be perfected or are mature to be thus minded. He gives an even greater encouragement: if you don't think this way, God will reveal it to you! What a good and gracious God! If I am not focused on the prize, He reveals it. If I am holding on to the past—wins, failures, victories, defeats, hurts—He will reveal those too. If I am wandering aimlessly toward my eternal destination for which He took hold of me, in His grace and mercy He reveals that too.

Then Paul reminds us, "Let us hold true to what we have attained" (Philippians 3:16). "Hold true" means "to exercise the mind; to give mental attention to; to be mentally disposed (more or less earnestly in a certain direction); intensively, to interest oneself in (with concern or obedience)—set the affection on, be careful with; be of the same mind; regard; think; savor."[1]

In short, Paul is saying, "You may not have obtained Christlikeness. I have not either. However, you have obtained the high, upward call in Christ, and you have obtained a greater measure of Christlikeness as you have matured. Think on this. Be careful with this. Give your mental energy to this. Savor this. Set your affection on this."

Pay attention to what you have obtained while fixing your attention on what you will obtain. Don't lose focus. Don't lose ground. Don't get sidetracked. Don't lose heart. We are all in the same race, but—thanks be to God—we are not in competition with each other. We are straining against ourselves and our own flesh. This is not a "second place is first loser" type of race. This is us, leaving our old selves in the dust as we strain toward the new "us" we will be in the resurrection.

TWENTY-NINE

That Day

IF MARTIN LUTHER WAS RIGHT, we only need to think about two days: this day and that day.[1] This day is the one you woke up to. This day is the gift of God intended for fruitful labor in His kingdom. This day is the only one we can do anything with.

That day is the day of Christ's return. That day is the day all creation groans for. That day is unknown. That day is the most important day in the future. We should be living with that day in mind: the day of our Lord Jesus Christ.

Paul lived with this glorious day of Jesus Christ on his mind. Much of what we know about it and our theology of the end comes from Paul's writings. We learn from him that at the last trumpet, we will all be raised, changed in the twinkling of an eye, and that we will be given new bodies (1 Corinthians 15:50–56). We learn from his teachings that judgment awaits on the day of the Lord and a crown of righteousness awaits those who have loved the Lord and His appearing (Romans 2:16; 2 Timothy 4:8). Both letters to the Thessalonians are distinctly teaching about that day of the Lord, correcting misinformation these believers had.

In Philippians 1, Paul provides a promise and a prayer regarding the day of Jesus. I am sure these were an encouragement and a blessing to the original readers, and they should be to us as well: "I thank my God in all my remembrance of you, always in every prayer of mine for you all making my prayer with joy, because of your partnership in the gospel from the first day until now. And I am sure of this, that he who began a good work in you will bring it to completion at the day of Jesus Christ" (Philippians 1:3–6). Oh, to be a finished work! I get frustrated with myself—whether my lack of growth, a persistent sin, my physical or mental limitations—and yearn to be better. I am annoyed at my own sin nature. I want to be complete: whole and spiritually mature. I want to be wise. I want to walk in the fullness of righteousness.

But I am not there yet. According to Paul, God will complete the work at the end. Completion is on His timescale, not mine. This lifts the burden of perfection I've felt has been errantly placed on me by my own expectations and from the church.

One of the more challenging aspects of growing up in the church is the lack of transparency from this incorrect expectation. For a long time, the church in America has projected an image of perfection that is unrealistic. I struggled—and I am sure a lot of others have as well—with security in my salvation because I did not meet this plastic, fake version of Christianity that I was seeing. I was drawn to authentic believers who let the rough edges show, who were honest about their struggles and weaknesses. They "let it all hang out" without glorying in their sin.

These honest believers strengthened my faith in the Jesus who sees all and knows all and can handle it. He isn't surprised by my sin or my shortcomings. He knows I have sins I turn to when I am stressed, sins that looks more enticing when I am tired, sins that beset me when I have a disagreement with someone. It was freeing to encounter believers who didn't hide their true selves from Christ or others.

This is the kind of authentic Christian I want to be. I will not be complete this side of eternity. I am growing. I am being transformed. I am becoming more Christlike. Why do I have to hide that I am still a work in progress from the other unfinished works?

A church parking lot on Sunday morning is an interesting place.

You can watch literal physical transformations take place when the car doors open. You can watch a couple scream and fight with each other as they pull into a parking spot, but magically turn into happy, smiling lovebirds when they open the car doors. I am sure the reverse transformation occurs when they return to the vehicle after service.

Why do we embrace such dishonesty as a culture? How much more could we grow if we came to church with our hurts and disappointments and bared them honestly? What if the couples who fight on the way to church sought out another couple who has more experience working out disagreements to help them? What if they stopped pretending that everything was perfect and just owned that they are incomplete masterpieces? How much of our growth or maturation as believers is stunted because we do not have the confidence in the work God is doing in our lives and in others to be real?

There is no such thing as a complete Christian this side of the resurrection.

And that is good news.

We can be sure, however, that God *began* to work in us when we received Jesus. When we became in Christ, we became a new creation. Legally speaking, our record was cleared, and we were right with God—square with the house—and our debt was cleared. God began right then the lifelong process of making us like Christ. If you like fancy theological terms, we have been justified and we are being sanctified. In the end, when we are complete, we will be glorified. All three of these terms are sealed in promise. They are sure.

The modern American church has given the wrong impression by pretending we are glorified while we are barely sanctified. The world looks at this error and calls us hypocrites, and rightly so. Hypocrites are pretenders, actors behind masks.

If we step out from behind the mask of perfection, our honesty is appealing. If I am struggling to overcome a sin, and I call it sin, ask for prayer and accountability to address the sin through God's grace, applying Scripture and relying on the transformative power of the Holy Spirit to work in me according to God's good pleasure, that is a far better witness than hiding my sin behind a screen of a carefully curated image of perfection. Like in *The Wizard of Oz*, a small thing like Toto can uncover the man behind the curtain and unveil my lies. We can only call out, "Pay no attention to the man behind the curtain!" so long before our testimony of God's greatness appears to be the illusion.[2]

God is so tender and gracious as He deals with the process of our becoming complete. I think our minds would explode if He revealed everything to us at once. Our hearts surely would fail under the strain if He opened our eyes to the totality of our sin in one sitting. He works slowly and methodically to build our trust in His promises, to reveal enough about Himself to give us deeper understanding, and to address each sin as we are ready.

To be sure, we have work to do. When we actively seek God, put to death what is earthly in us, obey Scripture, pray, practice the spiritual disciplines, and fellowship with other believers, God works in and through these things to bring about the part of completion and maturity that we will experience before death.

We should not have a fatalistic mind-set, however, thinking since we will always be incomplete, we do not have to grow. God's goal for you is spiritual maturity—Christlikeness—and you can experience it in increasing measures in this lifetime. Paul reminds the Corinthians in his second letter that we are the temple of God, He dwells with us, setting us apart, making us holy children. He concludes this thought with, "Since we have these promises, beloved, let us cleanse ourselves from every defilement of body and spirit, bringing holiness to completion in the fear of God" (2 Corinthians 7:1).

Your heart's desire should be to arrive at the finish line of your life as close to completion as possible. You should be a willing participant in the completing work God has begun in you.

Beloved, God keeps his promises. He does not lie. He does not go back on His word. He does not forget or get busy. He has promised us completion at the day of Jesus Christ. He will keep that promise. How glorious it will be to stand before Him at the throne as complete, whole, sanctified, pure, and righteous! Paul tells the Thessalonians, "Now may the God of peace himself sanctify you completely, and may your whole spirit and soul and body be kept blameless at the coming of our Lord Jesus Christ. He who calls you is faithful; he will surely do it" (1 Thessalonians 5:23–24). Similarly, Jude writes in his letter, "Now to him who is able to keep you from stumbling and to present you blameless before the presence of his glory with great joy, to the only God, our Savior, through Jesus Christ our Lord, be glory, majesty, dominion, and authority, before all time and now and forever. Amen" (Jude 1:24–25). Amen indeed!

Paul writes his letter to the Philippians with great affection. He expresses how they are on his mind and in his prayers and, in this final section, how they are in his heart. There is a deep sense of love and longing for their fullness in Christ throughout this letter. Paul often has a reputation for being so intellectual as to be not personable, but letters like this refute that assertion. He is connected and affectionate, warm and encouraging.

He writes,

> It is right for me to feel this way about you all, because I hold you in my heart, for you are all partakers with me of grace, both in my imprisonment and in the defense and confirmation of the gospel. For God is my witness, how I yearn for you all with the affection of Christ Jesus. And it is my prayer that your love may abound more and more, with knowledge and all discernment, so that you may approve what is excellent, and so be pure and blameless for the day of Christ, filled with the fruit of righteousness that comes through Jesus Christ, to the glory and praise of God. (Philippians 1:7–11)

When someone who loves me, someone who has invested in my life, who knows my heart, gives me a word of advice, I *listen*. As Paul expresses his love for these believers, I find myself drawn in. I want to hear what he is going to tell them. As he reiterates his love and affection for them, I hear my own heart saying, *Listen up! This is important!*

"It is my prayer that your love may abound more and more."

Paul prays for them to have more and more *agape* love specifically, that it would excel still more, to increase in excellence. Abound can be used to describe a flower going from bud to full bloom. That's a great word picture! Your love should bloom.

Note that Paul doesn't give an object for the love. Just the type: Christlike, benevolent affection, brotherly love, charity.

But he does give a few qualifiers: "with knowledge and all discernment." The word for knowledge means "precise and correct knowledge," while discernment means "perception, not just of the senses but of the intellect."[3] Beloved, we are to grow in our knowledge of Jesus, and we need to be sure it is precise and correct knowledge. We live in a day and age where the only prerequisite for an opinion is to have a platform. Careful study of the Bible, research, and systematic theology have been replaced with emotional responses, clever videos, and ear-tickling nuance. You must undertake a careful study of the Bible for yourself if you are to have an abounding love with knowledge and discernment.

Discernment is the ability to judge between matters. If two ideologies are presented to you, discernment is looking at them with the intellect to figure out which is truth. Sadly, most Christians today are following their feelings and emotions rather than their intellect. We are not students of the Word, but rather students of our own gut. We need to know the word to discern what is biblically true.

We learn about God through the careful, consistent reading of His Word, the Bible. Reading what others say, taking Bible study classes, and listening to sermons are all good things, but they are not enough. If all I knew of my husband was what other people said of him, how strong would our relationship be? In terms of human relationships, we would say we "know about" someone if we know information regarding them from other sources. We *know* someone when the information comes from them personally and we have an ongoing relationship with them.

It is crucial that we know God personally and intimately as we journey toward the goal of contentment. If I am to trust God, I want to have as close to an accurate picture of Him as I can. I want to know that the God in whom I am finding satisfaction is capable of satisfying my soul. If I am going to rely on someone, I want to know they are reliable. I want to read for myself how the holy King worked on behalf of His subjects. If I am trusting in His goodness and mercy, I need to have knowledge of what that means as He has revealed it through His Word. If I am placing my faith in a half-baked idea of the God I serve, I will only be relying on my own half-baked notions. I want to depend on God as He is, not as I imagine Him to be.

I never run out of things to learn about God! Every time I read through the Bible, I see things I have never seen before; I learn a historical fact that puts something in new light; I learn something about myself that makes a verse jump off the page in a new way. I think I could live to be a thousand years old and study every day without fully understanding God. He is so good and gracious to reveal as much as we can understand in each increment of our growth.

Paul gives us the "why" for abounding love in knowledge and discernment, the "so that . . ." in verses 10–11.

First, "you may approve what is excellent" (Philippians 1:10). You may test, examine, prove, scrutinize, as in seeing if a thing is genuine or not, what is good and lawful as opposed to evil or unlawful. When we abound in love based on knowledge and discernment, we are better able to determine right and wrong, with a desire to do right because of our love.

Second, we can "be pure and blameless for the day of Christ" (Philippians 1:10). This word for "pure" means "judged by sunlight," as in tested as genuine, pure, sincere. If you were held up in the bright sunlight, would your faith be proved genuine? Blameless is just that: blameless, not led into sin. By abounding in love more and more, growing in knowledge and discernment, examining things to see if they are good or evil, we will be more and more drawn to the things that delight the Lord, and as a result we will become pure and blameless. We will *want* Him to find us as complete as possible on that day.

Third, we are to be "filled with the fruit of righteousness that comes through Jesus Christ" (Philippians 1:11). Filled! Oh, what a wonderful word! To make full, liberally supplied, abounding, full to the brim! Figuratively, *fruit* means works, acts, or deeds. Can you imagine so being filled with the righteousness from Jesus that you are overflowing with good deeds? I *long* for the day when all I think, say, and do is righteous! Can you imagine always knowing what is right and good and choosing that out of love and devotion to Jesus? This is Paul's prayer for these believers!

Finally, we can strive to do all "to the glory and praise of God" (Philippians 1:11). Here we are at the chief end of man, to glorify God. It brings glory to God when His people abound in love in increasing measure, with knowledge and discernment. It glorifies God when His children test everything and follow good over evil, when they are pure and blameless in this life and long for "that day," when they are filled with the fruit of righteousness from His Son. God is praised and glorified when we live from a place of loving Him above all else, so much that we forsake all else for His glory. Other people see our love for Him—and by extension our love for them—and how we are different, and they will learn to glorify God through us. Jesus said, "In the same way, let your light shine before others, so that they may see your good works and give glory to your Father who is in heaven" (Matthew 5:16).

This is what the quest for contentment is about: glorifying God. As I make much of God in my own life—being satisfied in Him, quieted by His love, confident in His care and provision—I begin to have an otherworldly response to the world around me. I am unruffled by the circumstances I face. I am at peace when my world is in turmoil. I am confident in the face of persecution and unflappable in times of trial. People pay attention.

Paul was the picture of contentment for the sake of the gospel. He lived with that end in mind, and in the end it transformed his mind. He was immovable in purpose. Because Christ was everything to Paul, who counted it a privilege to suffer for Christ's sake, Paul accepted everything from God's hand as for his good and the advancement of the gospel. Our aim in seeking Paul-like contentment should be Paul-like resolve and dedication. Our purpose should be to see as many come to the Lord as possible through our peaceful dependence on God's loving-kindness.

When I was growing up, there was a catchy praise chorus we sang with the refrain, "Thy loving-kindness is better than life." Years later, I discovered the psalm it was based on. Psalm 63 has become my anthem in searching for contentment. Read carefully the words of David:

> O God, you are my God; earnestly I seek you;
>> my soul thirsts for you;
>> my flesh faints for you,
>> as in a dry and weary land where there is no water.
>> So I have looked upon you in the sanctuary,
>> beholding your power and glory.
>> Because your steadfast love is better than life,
>> my lips will praise you.
>> So I will bless you as long as I live;
>> in your name I will lift up my hands.
>
> My soul will be satisfied as with fat and rich food,
>> and my mouth will praise you with joyful lips,
>> when I remember you upon my bed,
>> and meditate on you in the watches of the night;
>> for you have been my help,
>> and in the shadow of your wings I will sing for joy.
>> My soul clings to you;
>> your right hand upholds me. (Psalm 63:1–8)

David's longing for God's presence is active and tangible. Hunger, thirst, longing fill his thoughts. His prayers echo both satisfaction in and clinging to the Lord. He knows the steadfast love of the Lord is better than life.

God reveals Himself to Moses as, "The LORD, the LORD, a God merciful and gracious, slow to anger, and abounding in steadfast love and faithfulness" (Exodus 34:6–7). Our God abounds in steadfast love and faithfulness. In Hebrew, the word for steadfast love is *hesed*.[4] This is one of those words that gets lost in translation. No one English word can grasp the richness of this Hebrew word. It is

197

loving-kindness, mercy, goodness, goodliness, favor, faithfulness all in one. It is God's *hesed* love that endures forever, works on our behalf, sustains us, saves us, forgives us, cleanses us, redeems us, brings us into covenant with Him and keeps us in that covenant, does not forsake us. His steadfast love extends to the heavens, and His mercy reaches to the clouds.

Indeed, this steadfast love is better than life. This is the source of contentment. I need to believe this deep down in my soul, with every fiber of my being. I need to say as David did, "Your steadfast love is before my eyes, and I walk in your faithfulness" (Psalm 26:3).

I need to fix my eyes upon His steadfast love and faithfulness because I am not steadfast or faithful. I can often love this world more than I love Him. And I certainly love myself more than Him or my neighbor. I am fickle, temperamental, and as prone to shifting opinions as waves are prone to crash upon the shore. If I am going to be content, especially in terms of being completed in eternity, I need to find my contentment in God's unchanging, sure, steadfast nature, not my own fleeting emotions and moods. I need to look to His *hesed* love and faithfulness.

The writer of Hebrews also reminds us of God's steadfastness but uses the Greek word transliterated *bebaios*, meaning stable, sure, firm, steadfast.[5] He pairs it with the word *asphalaes*, which means not fail, secure, certain, sure.[6] Here is the verse they are combined in: "We have this as a sure and steadfast anchor for the soul, a hope that enters into the inner place behind the curtain, where Jesus has gone as a forerunner on our behalf" (Hebrews 6:19–20).

Beloved, Jesus has already gone where we aim to go. He is there on our behalf. He has given us His promises, which are both sure and steadfast. Our souls are to be anchored to His ability to keep His promises. He cannot—and will not—fail us. Jesus completed His work on earth and sat down at the right hand of the Father. He promises to complete His work in us and bring us to our eternal destination in the Father's presence.

Oh, how much grief I have brought upon myself because I have not fully trusted His promises! I have been afraid of death because of my lack of trust. Consider the words Paul uses to comfort Timothy as Paul approaches his end: "The saying is trustworthy, for: if we have died with him, we will also live with him; if we endure, we will also reign with him; if we deny him; he also will deny us; if we are faithless, he remains faithful—for he cannot deny himself." (2 Timothy 2:11–13).

God has promised me eternal life because I have put my faith in Jesus Christ. He will keep His promise. He is faithful. He is sure. I can be content in Him because He cannot deny Himself. We can follow the instructions the writer wrote to the Hebrews to run our race with endurance, laying aside every weight and sin that could trip us up or hinder us, "looking to Jesus the founder and perfecter of our faith" (Hebrews 12:1–2). He is our example, guarantor, mediator, and prize. Our souls are firmly anchored in hope to His sure and steadfast self. Oh, how good He is!

Friends, this pursuit of contentment thus far has been the most rewarding spiritual challenge I have undertaken in my walk with Christ. I hope and pray you have seen a glimpse of the possibility to have complete and total satisfaction in God. I pray this book has awoken in you a longing for deep, utter stillness of soul flowing from peace with God.

In the movie adaptation on J.R.R. Tolkien's *The Lord of the Rings: The Fellowship of the Ring*, shortly after the movie begins, Bilbo Baggins quits Bag End for one last adventure, leaving behind the Shire, Frodo, and the ring. He takes a few steps out the door, then looks back at his trusty friend Gandalf. "I have thought of an ending to my book," Bilbo tells him. "'And he lived happily ever after to the end of his days.'"[7]

And here we are, at the end of our book, ready to embark on our adventure of pursuing contentment. May you live contentedly to the end of your days. Until *that* day, may we all find our satisfaction in God, trusting in Him for all things, doing all things—particularly being content—through Him who strengthens us.

Notes

Introduction

1. Matthew George Easton, ed., *Easton's Bible Dictionary*, 3rd ed., n.p., 1897, Blue Letter Bible.com, accessed June 19, 2022, https://www.blueletterbible.org/search/dictionary /viewTopic.cfm?topic=ET0000888,NT0001211,ST0000036, TT0000121.
2. Jeremiah Burroughs, *The Rare Jewel of Christian Contentment* (London: Henry G. Bohn, 1645), loc. 313 of 3723, Kindle.
3. Burroughs, *The Rare Jewel of Christian Contentment*, loc. 418 of 3723, Kindle.
4. Burroughs, *The Rare Jewel of Christian Contentment*, loc. 128 of 3723, Kindle.
5. Thomas Watson, *The Art of Divine Contentment*, rev. by Jason Roth (n.p.: Christian Classics for the Modern Reader, 2017), loc. 254 of 3234, Kindle.
6. Watson, *The Art of Divine Contentment*, loc. 1028 of 3234, Kindle.
7. Burroughs, *The Rare Jewel of Christian Contentment*, loc. 735 of 3723, Kindle.

4. Paul's Encouragement

1. Saul McLeod, "Maslow's Hierarchy of Needs," *Simply Psychology*, published 2007, updated April 4, 2022, https://www.simplypsychology.org/maslow.html.

6. Circumstances Expose Sin

1. "Mal-," Dictionary.com, accessed March 12, 2022, https://www.dictionary.com/browse/mal-.

8. Circumstances Teach Us Endurance and Steadfastness

1. "Steadfast," *Webster's Ninth New Collegiate Dictionary* (Springfield, Mass: Merriam-Webster, 1983).

9. Circumstances Change Our Perspective

1. Hope Babowice, "Jupiter, Fifth from the Sun and 300 Times Larger than Earth," *Daily Herald*, August 5, 2019, accessed March 7, 2022, https://www.dailyherald.com/submitted /20190805/jupiter-fifth-from-the-sun-and-300-times-larger-than-earth.

2. Daisy Dobrijevic and Tim Sharp, "How Big Is the Moon?" Space.com, January 28, 2022, accessed March 7, 2022, https://www.space.com/18135-how-big-is-the-moon.html; Tim Sharp and Ailsa Harvey, "How Big Is the Sun?" Space.com, January 21, 2022, accessed March 7, 2022, https://www.space.com/17001-how-big-is-the-sun-size-of-the-sun.html.
3. Nikolaus Zinzendorf, TheMajestysMen.com, accessed March 8, 2022, https://the-majestysmen.com/quotes/nikolaus-zinzendorf-forgotten-quote/.
4. Jim Elliot, BrainyQuote.com, accessed March 8, 2022, https://www.brainyquote.com /quotes/jim_elliot _189244.

11. Responding to Your Circumstances (Part 2)

1. Jeremiah Burroughs, *The Rare Jewel of Christian Contentment* (London: Henry G. Bohn, 1645), loc. 431 of 3723, Kindle.
2. Burroughs, *The Rare Jewel of Christian Contentment*, loc. 391 of 3723, Kindle.
3. Thomas Watson, *The Art of Divine Contentment*, rev. by Jason Roth (n.p.: Christian Classics for the Modern Reader, 2017), loc. 1176 of 3234, Kindle.

12. The Guarded Heart and Mind

1. "Noéma," *Strong's Concordance*, Blue Letter Bible.com, accessed June 19, 2022, https://www.blueletterbible.org/lexicon/g3540/esv/mgnt/0-1/.
2. "Epieikēs," *Strong's Concordance*, Blue Letter Bible.com, accessed June 18, 2022, https://www.blueletterbible.org/lexicon/g1933/esv/mgnt/0-1/.

13. Do Not Be Anxious

1. Charles Spurgeon, *John Ploughman's Talk* (Philadelphia: Henry Altemus Company, 1896), 80.

16. Think on These (Part 1)

1. "Semnos," *Strong's Concordance*, Blue Letter Bible.com, accessed June 19, 2022, https://www.blueletterbible.org/lexicon/g4586/esv/mgnt/0-1/.
2. "August," Thesaurus.com, accessed March 12, 2022, https://www.thesaurus.com/browse/august; "honorable," accessed March 12, 2022, https://www.thesaurus.com/browse/honorable; "reverend," accessed March 12, 2022, https://www.thesaurus.com/browse/reverend; "venerable," accessed March 12, 2022, https://www.thesaurus.com/browse/venerable. Also, "august," "honorable," "reverend," "venerable," *Webster's Ninth New Collegiate Dictionary* (Springfield, MA: Merriam-Webster, 1985), 579, 116, 1009, 1308.

17. Think on These (Part 2)

1. "Prosphilés," *Strong's Concordance*, Blue Letter Bible.com, accessed June 19, 2022, https://www.blueletterbible.org/lexicon/g4375/esv/mgnt/0-1/.
2. "Commendable," *Strong's Concordance*, Blue Letter Bible.com, accessed March 9, 2022, https://www.blueletterbible.org/lexicon/g2163/kjv/tr/0-1/.
3. Nancy Wilson, *Virtuous: A Study for Ladies of Every Age* (Moscow, ID: Canon Press, 2016), loc. 9 of 1159, Kindle.

24. The Christian Community

1. Martin Luther, *Luther's Works*, ed., Jaroslar Pelikan, v. 21 (St. Louis, MO: Concordia, 1956), 303.
2. "Philippi," *World History Encyclopedia*, accessed March 12, 2022, https://www.worldhistory.org/Philippi/; "Philip II," *Britannica*, accessed March 12, 2022, https://www.britannica.com/biography/Philip-II-king-of-Macedonia; http://www.ldolphin.org/pphilippi.html.

25. Three Examples

1. John Bunyan, *Pilgrim's Progress*, rev. by Alan Vermilye (n.p.: Brown Chair Books, 2020), loc. 1638 of 3531, Kindle.
2. Jeremiah Burroughs, *The Rare Jewel of Christian Contentment* (London: Henry G. Bohn, 1645), loc. 1366 of 3723, Kindle.

26. Community Responsibilities

1. "Katergazomai," *Strong's Concordance*, Blue Letter Bible.com, accessed June 19, 2022, https://www.blueletterbible.org/lexicon/g2716/esv/mgnt/0-1/.
2. "Tromos," *Strong's Concordance*, Blue Letter Bible.com, accessed March 12, 2022, https://www.blueletterbible.org/lexicon/g5156/kjv/tr/0-1/.
3. Jeremiah Burroughs, *The Rare Jewel of Christian Contentment* (London: Henry G. Bohn, 1645), loc. 418 of 3723, Kindle.
4. Burroughs, loc. 391 of 3723, Kindle.
5. "Skolios," *Strong's Concordance*, BlueLetterBible.com, accessed June 18, 2022, https://www.blueletterbible.org/lexicon/g4646/kjv/tr/0-1/.
6. "Diastrephō," *Strong's Concordance*, BlueLetterBible.com, accessed June 18, 2022, https://www.blueletterbible.org/lexicon/g1294/kjv/tr/0-1/.

27. Paul's Desire

1. John Piper, *Don't Waste Your Life* (Wheaton, IL: Crossway, 2003), 64.
2. Charles Spurgeon, "10 Spurgeon Quotes on Dying Well," *The Spurgeon Center*, June 29, 2017, accessed March 7, 2022, https://www.spurgeon.org/resource-library/blog-entries/10-spurgeon-quotes-on-dying-well/.

28. Not Yet

1. "Phroneō," *Strong's Concordance*, BlueLetterBible.com, accessed March 12, 2022, https://www.blueletterbible.org/lexicon/g5426/kjv/tr/0-1/.

29. That Day

1. Martin Luther, AZQuotes.com, accessed March 7, 2022, https://www.azquotes.com/quote /395602.

2. *The Wizard of Oz,* directed by Victor Fleming, written by Noel Langley, Florence Ryerson, and Edgar Allen Woolf, featuring Judy Garland, Grank Morgan, Ray Boler, et al. (Beverly Hills, CA: Metro-Goldwyn-Mayer, 1939), 1:34:45.

3. "Epignōsis," *Strong's Concordance*, BlueLetterBible.com, accessed March 12, 2022, https://www.blueletterbible.org/lexicon/g1922/esv/mgnt/0-1/; "Aisthēsis," *Strong's Concordance*, BlueLetterBible.com, accessed March 12, 2022, https://www.blueletterbible.org/lexicon/g144/esv/mgnt/0-1/.

4. "Hesed," *Strong's Concordance*, BlueLetterBible.com, accessed March 12, 2022, https://www.blueletterbible.org/lexicon/h2617/esv/wlc/0-1/.

5. "Bebaios," *Strong's Concordance*, BlueLetterBible.com, accessed June 19, 2022, https://www.blueletterbible.org/lexicon/g949/esv/mgnt/0-1/.

6. "Asphalés," *Strong's Concordance*, BlueLetterBible.com, accessed June 19, 2022, https://www.blueletterbible.org/lexicon/g804/esv/mgnt/0-1/.

7. *The Lord of the Rings: The Fellowship of the Ring,* directed by Peter Jackson, written by Fran Walsh and Philippa Boyens, featuring Barrie Osborne, Peter Jackson, Fran Walsh, Howard Shore, Elijah Wood, Ian McKellen, Liv Tyler, et al., based on J.R.R. Tolkien's *The Lord of the Rings: The Fellowship of the Ring* (Los Angeles: New Line Home Entertainment, 2001), 29:10.